The Architecture of James Gamble Rogers II in Winter Park, Florida

UNIVERSITY PRESS OF FLORIDA

Florida A&M University, Tallahassee
Florida Atlantic University, Boca Raton
Florida Gulf Coast University, Ft. Myers
Florida International University, Miami
Florida State University, Tallahassee
New College of Florida, Sarasota
University of Central Florida, Orlando
University of Florida, Gainesville
University of North Florida, Jacksonville
University of South Florida, Tampa
University of West Florida, Pensacola

The Architecture of

JAMES GAMBLE ROGERS II

in Winter Park, Florida

Patrick W. McClane and Debra A. McClane

University Press of Florida
Gainesville
Tallahassee
Tampa
Boca Raton
Pensacola
Orlando
Miami
Jacksonville
Ft. Myers
Sarasota

First cloth printing, 2004
First paperback printing, 2023

27 26 25 24 23   5 4 3 2 1

A record of cataloging-in-publication data is available from the Library of Congress.
ISBN 978-0-8130-2770-8 (cloth)
ISBN 978-0-8130-8037-6 (pbk.)

Frontispiece: Barbour house, ca. 1933. Harold Haliday Costain. Courtesy of RLF.
Title page: James Gamble Rogers II, ca. 1984. Courtesy of RLF.
Repeated efforts were made to obtain written permission
to reprint plate 12.

The University Press of Florida is the scholarly publishing agency for the State
University System of Florida, comprising Florida A&M University, Florida Atlantic
University, Florida Gulf Coast University, Florida International University, Florida
State University, New College of Florida, University of Central Florida, University
of Florida, University of North Florida, University of South Florida, and University
of West Florida.

University Press of Florida
2046 NE Waldo Road
Suite 2100
Gainesville, FL 32609
http://upress.ufl.edu

Ode to Daybreak

A breeze blows slowly and lazily by
   That comes from the heart of the deep,
And out of the woodlands the nightingale's cry
   Tells that the world is asleep;
 There's a call from the stars and a call from the sea,
   And as I take leave of the shore
There is not a sound o'er the crest of the deep
   Save the dip of my own muffled oar.

As I paddle along o'er the glistening waves
   There appears in the path of the moon
A black-shrouded ship, but e'er I look twice
   It's mingled with Darkness too soon;
My wakefulness ends when the breath of the dawn
   Comes forth from the dying moonbeams,
And yielding to Somnus, I finish my cruise
   In the beautiful garden of dreams.

—J. G. Rogers II, '18
Poem by Rogers that appeared in *The Sentinel*,
his senior yearbook at Daytona Beach High School, 1918.

Contents

List of Figures   ix

List of Black and White Plates   xi

List of Color Plates   xiii

Preface   xv

1. The Rogers Family   1

2. Beginning in Winter Park   17

3. Developing an Architectural Character in Winter Park   44

4. The Legacy   51

5. Selected Houses   56

   Rogers House (1929)   56

   Shippen House (1931)   62

   Barbour House (1932)   69

   Barbour Apartments (1938)   82

   Noyes House (1934)   85

   McAllaster House (1934)   91

   Harris House (ca. 1936)   100

   Holt House (1937)   103

   Jewett House (1937)   107

   Leonard House (1937)   111

   Burress House (1939)   117

   Plant House (1939)   121

   Mizener House (1939)   124

Appendix. Catalogue of Residential Work   131

Notes   153

Bibliography   161

Index   165

Figures

1. Map of Winter Park, 1888   19

2. Rogers house, first floor plan   59

3. Rogers house, west elevation   61

4. Shippen house, first floor plan   66

5. Barbour house, first floor plan   71

6. Noyes house, first floor plan   89

7. McAllaster house, first floor plan   92

8. Harris house, north elevation   100

9. Harris house, first floor plan   101

10. Harris house, east elevation   102

11. Holt house, first floor plan, 1937   105

12. Holt house, first floor plan, 1941   106

13. Jewett house, second floor plan   108

14. Leonard house, south elevation   114

15. Leonard house, north elevation   114

16. Burress house, first floor plan   120

17. Plant house, first floor plan   123

18. Mizener house, first floor plan   127

19. Huttig house, east elevation   131

Black and White Plates

1. James Gamble Rogers I, ca. 1890   3

2. Harkness Tower, Yale University   6

3. John Arthur Rogers, ca. 1912   10

4. James Gamble Rogers as a student at Dartmouth College   13

5. 1924 Dartmouth swimming team   14

6. Rogers as captain of swimming team   14

7. Evelyn Claire Smith and James Gamble Rogers at their engagement party   16

8. Park Avenue, looking east, ca. 1888   18

9. The "old" Seminole Hotel, 1896   19

10. Victor N. Camp house, Ormond Beach, 1928   22

11. Fern Park Post Office Building, ca. 1930   23

12. Advertisement for A. T. Traylor house, 1930   24

13. James Gamble Rogers II house on Isle of Sicily, 1930   25

14. The *Caprice* and part of her crew after the 1938 hurricane   29

15. The Rogers family and Vicky on the steps of their home in Temple Grove, 1948   30

16. Rendering of Mills Library, Rollins College   32

17. Olin Library, Rollins College   33

18. Florida Supreme Court Building, Tallahassee, 1946   39

19. Rogers in front of Olin Library, 1986   42

20. L. V. Bledsoe house, 1940   47

21. Rogers on the *Lotus*   54

22. Rogers house, lakeside facade   57

23. Shippen house, interior courtyard   65

24. Shippen house, north facade   67

25. Barbour house, view to east   69

26. Barbour house, view to northeast 73

27. Barbour house, detail of pointed arch 73

28. Barbour house, front balcony and turret 74

29. Barbour house, view from second-story balcony 75

30. Barbour house, detail of broken arches 76

31. Barbour house, view looking northwest at arched loggia 76

32. Barbour house, entrance hall 77

33. Barbour house, north wall of living room 78

34. Barbour house, interior courtyard 79

35. Barbour house, living room 81

36. Barbour Apartments, view to southeast 84

37. Noyes house, view to northwest 85

38. Noyes house, courtyard and turret 87

39. Noyes house, detail of window grille 88

40. Noyes house, detail of front door 90

41. McAllaster house, view to east 91

42. McAllaster house, loggia entryway 93

43. McAllaster house, courtyard 94

44. McAllaster house, view from second-story balcony 97

45. Ingram house, view to southwest 98

46. Ingram house, detail of doorway 98

47. Ingram house, detail of arched openings into cloister 99

48. Jewett house, detail of entry 109

49. Jewett house, upstairs living room 110

50. Leonard house, view to northwest 112

51. Leonard house, view from outdoor terrace toward dining room 115

52. Leonard house, stair column and light fixture 116

53. Burress house, detail of half-timbering 119

54. Keene house, view to northeast 129

Color Plates

Following page 76

1. Greeneda Court, Park Avenue, Winter Park
2. Shippen house, view to northeast
3. Shippen house, view of stair hall
4. Holt house, east facade
5. Holt house, detail of east facade
6. Holt house, living room
7. Jewett house, view to northeast
8. Burress house, view to southwest
9. Burress house, view to north
10. Burress house, living room
11. Plant house, view to southeast
12. Plant house, living room
13. Mizener house, view to north
14. Mizener house, stair hall

Preface

In 1993 we were awarded the inaugural Rhea Marsh Smith and Dorothy Lockhart Smith Research Grant, which was jointly sponsored by the Olin Library at Rollins College and the Winter Park Public Library. The aim of the annual grant is to promote scholarly research on some historical aspect of Winter Park, Florida. Our topic, the residential architecture of James Gamble Rogers II in Winter Park, proved to be a larger matter than we first imagined. Rogers' long career included many commissions, and a study of his work required separating actual Rogers works from those that were reputedly by the architect. There were magazine articles to review, office files and project drawings to study, and owners and former owners to interview. The nearly 100-page manuscript submitted was the culmination of many hours of researching, interviewing, photographing, and writing. Copies of the manuscript were submitted to both sponsoring libraries and, at the conclusion of the project, we presented a lecture on the topic at the Winter Park Public Library and at the Woman's Club of Winter Park. Still, we felt that the information we had compiled would be appealing to a wider audience. Through publication of this book, we hope to reach that audience.

This publication is the first to focus solely on the work of James Gamble Rogers II. Rogers' designs have been featured in local newspapers and magazines and were represented in two chapters of Richard N. Campen's *Winter Park Portrait: The Story of Winter Park and Rollins College*, which is the most complete published architectural history of the city. More recently, Robin Chapman featured Rogers' architecture in *The Absolutely Essential Guide to Winter Park*, which was well illustrated with historical postcards and photographs. Both Campen and Chapman credited Rogers with having had more influence on the style and quality of Winter Park's domestic architecture than perhaps any other single individual.

In this first book devoted solely to Rogers, we have included biographical information on the architect and his family that is useful in understanding Rogers' participation in the development of Florida's architectural character, particularly in Winter Park. The last chapter of the book is a review and analysis of thirteen Rogers designs, reconstructing the conditions of each commission, with biographical information on the clients to the extent possible. The main sources for this section include Rogers' sketches, working drawings, personal library, writings, and office files. Site visits and interviews with owners and associated individuals have supplemented this information. Many of the residences were featured in regional and national architectural magazines, indicating professional acceptance and admiration of Rogers' work.

The residential designs presented here were completed prior to World War II. While this may seem a narrow view of an architectural career that spanned nearly seventy years and that also included a large number of institutional and governmental designs, it is in his early residential portfolio that we most clearly see Rogers' genius for designing intriguing and inspiring spaces that exhibit a well-honed sense of proportion and style. In fact, if Rogers' career had ended before he was forty—a creative milestone for many notable architects—he would still be remembered as an image maker for Winter Park, and his work would still warrant praise and study.

In the discussions of individual houses, we have attempted to develop, as much as possible, the cultural and social context of each commission. Since no building can be fully understood outside of its context, this information lends a deeper appreciation of the final product. Many of these residences were built for Northerners newly arrived in Florida or for seasonal residents who sought to give shape to their and others' romantic ideas of Florida and the tropics. These residences were also intended to make a social statement about the status of their inhabitants, though they were not often executed on the scale of Addison Mizner's Palm Beach mansions. Though the larger commissions are the more well known of Rogers' designs, he also designed modest homes for businessmen, artists, and professors, examples of which are also included to illustrate the ease with which Rogers was able to perform for different clients of different means, while still providing an equally satisfying product.

Within these designs we see Rogers' response to the specific requirements of his clients, as well as to natural elements such as siting and the heat and humidity of Florida. We also see Rogers' response to contemporary trends in architecture and the stylistic choices made by the architect. Proficient in many styles, Rogers is best known for his Spanish Eclectic examples. However, Rogers also completed many Colonial Revival designs and even an International Style residence, though he does not seem to have admired Modernist architecture very much. In each of these designs, we see a blending of practical needs with aesthetic desires.

While Rogers is presented here as a regional architect, he clearly was not working within a vacuum. The early twentieth century, especially the prosperous decade after World War I, was a time of exceptional development in the United States, felt most acutely in Florida's explosive land boom, which was aided by the railroads of Henry Flagler along the east coast and Henry Plant along the west coast. The architectural style of Flagler's first St. Augustine hotel, the Ponce de Leon, reflected the Spanish roots of the resort town, though the famous architects of the building, John Carrère and Thomas Hastings, added touches of Moorish and Renaissance architecture into the mix. Flagler's hotels further south, including Carrère and Hastings' 1894 Royal Poinciana in Palm Beach, however, were shingle and clapboard structures with Colonial Revival details that were more appropriate to northern shores than to the Florida semitropics. Even Flagler's own home, known as Whitehall, reflected the brilliant white Beaux-Arts Classical Revival style of architecture that was transplanted from popular designs for Newport cottages. This trend changed in 1918, when Addison Mizner, another influential Florida architect, arrived in Palm Beach. For the next decade Mizner designed large seasonal mansions for some of the nation's wealthiest individuals, many of whom owned houses in both Newport and Palm Beach, and nearly single-handedly reshaped the image of Palm Beach architecture into the Mediterranean-inspired town we think of today.

In *Mizner's Florida*, Donald W. Curl illuminates the career of the architect whose work is described as "historicizing eclecticism" and who was fluent in Venetian, Spanish, and Latin American architectural styles, thus integrating the influences of many places and time periods within one design. Rogers could scarcely have been unaware of the work of Mizner, whose initial commission in Florida, the well-publicized Everglades Club in Palm Beach (1918), was the first major building in South Florida designed in the Spanish style. Other Florida architects, including Marion Sims Wyeth and Joseph Urban in Palm Beach and Richard Kiehnel and John M. Elliott in Miami, followed Mizner's lead in drawing on resplendent Mediterranean and Spanish influences to create notable residences and public buildings that others sought to emulate and that clients, no doubt, requested.

By 1929, when Rogers designed his own home, Four Winds, in Winter Park, Mizner's career was nearly finished, and his dream for the new development of Boca Raton had collapsed. Mizner's last large commission was completed in 1931, and by 1933 the architect was dead. Yet as Rogers embarked on his independent architectural career, much local and national architectural activity caught his attention and influenced some of his designs. None of Rogers' writings or interviews indicates that he was influenced by any one architect in particular, but his files are full of magazine clippings of designs and details in a myriad of historical styles. As with many architects, architectural and professional publications of the time were an important source for ideas and inspiration.

Rogers also was active in the local and state American Institute of Architects (AIA) and also participated in urban planning conferences. He was a founding member and the first president of the Mid-Florida chapter of the AIA and was a four-term president of the Florida State Board of Architecture (1940–1944). His professional library indicates that he was absorbing information from published books, journals, and popular magazines on the "exactness" of detailing Spanish homes, Colonial homes, and even French country homes. His keen ability to learn through observation was the primary self-educational tool that Rogers utilized throughout his career.

We have included in an appendix a catalogue of Rogers' residential projects. This list, while not exhaustive, is the most comprehensive to date and is compiled from actual drawings and office files. We have been careful to list only those works that can be confirmed by these primary resources. Continued research will certainly produce additions to the catalogue, but at more than 270 entries covering nearly seventy years, the list is already impressive in its scope. A handful of these residences are listed in the Florida Bureau of Historic Resources' statewide inventory of historic sites, and only a few of those have been placed in the National Register of Historic Places. This limited recognition is not because the buildings lack integrity or significance, but because the initiative has not yet been undertaken. The City of Winter Park has recently enacted a historic preservation ordinance that established the Winter Park Register of Historic Places. The program has resulted in the voluntary designation of nearly a dozen properties as local landmarks. This is a prudent first step in recognizing and protecting the city's important architectural treasures, but only personal interest in these buildings will protect them in the future. By recognizing their intrinsic value and the importance each plays in the larger tapestry of Winter Park's architecture, individuals will ultimately control whether these houses remain standing.

The passage of time between our original manuscript and the publication of this book has allowed us an opportunity to rewrite and reword passages, to add information, to correct errors of fact, and to benefit from other research conducted on this topic. Aaron Betsky's monograph on James Gamble Rogers I, Rogers' uncle and namesake, has proven helpful in rounding out the biographical information on the Rogers family. Individual homeowners and other historians have stepped forward to call our attention to many of Rogers' works. In addition, the Rogers family has been generous with personal papers, mementos, and memories.

We have many people to thank for their assistance in the completion of this book. We owe a great deal of gratitude to the architectural firm of Rogers, Lovelock, and Fritz (RLF), in particular John H. Rogers, president of the firm and son of James Gamble Rogers II, and Betty Spangler, executive assistant, without whom the completion of this book would not have been possible. Thanks also to Rob Ramsey of RLF, who assisted in gathering historical images of Rogers' works. The librarians and special collections archivists at Rollins College, especially Gertrude F. Laframbroise, have been helpful in providing copies of local architectural and social magazines. These historical images have been augmented by the artistic contemporary photographs provided by Rich Franco of Fotofactory. Finally, we would like to thank the many homeowners who allowed us to photograph and examine the houses included in this book. Their generosity is much appreciated.

1

The Rogers Family

JAMES GAMBLE ROGERS II came from a family of architects. His father, John Arthur Rogers, as well as his uncle, James Gamble Rogers I, were both successful architects in Chicago, New York, and Florida. According to an interview Rogers gave with the Morse Foundation, even his grandfather, Joseph Martin Rogers, had dabbled in architecture after he retired from his work as an attorney.[1] The elder Rogers, finding that he had considerable time on his hands and perhaps enticed by the fact that two of his sons had gone into the architectural profession, enrolled in a correspondence course, possibly through the American School of Correspondence, which was headquartered in Chicago.[2] He passed the Illinois state examination at the age of sixty, but executed no known designs except for his own residence in Seabreeze, Florida, located north of Daytona Beach, on Florida's Atlantic coast, where he wintered for twenty years.[3] It is evident that the younger Rogers learned from his uncle's and his father's examples and was greatly influenced by them in his approach to architecture, clients, and his professional and civic roles in shaping the world around him. An examination of this architectural lineage provides a basis for understanding the architectural career of James Gamble Rogers II.

James Gamble Rogers I (1867–1947)

James Gamble Rogers I, FAIA, was born on March 3, 1867, in Bryant's Station, Kentucky, outside of Lexington. Gamble, as he was known, grew up in Buena Park, a suburb on the north side of Chicago. Although the Rogers family had been in Kentucky since 1784, when Gamble's great-grandfather, Joseph Hale Rogers (ca. 1742–1834), arrived from Culpeper County, Virginia, Gamble's father, Joseph Martin Rogers (1839–1923), moved the family to Chicago during Reconstruction, no doubt seeking better economic conditions than were available in Bryant's Station.[4]

James Gamble Rogers I attended Chicago public schools, graduating from high school in 1885. He then attended Yale University on scholarship, where he made lasting friendships that would later influence his career. The young Rogers became editor of the undergraduate magazine and was a member and manager of the baseball team. In his junior year he was tapped for election into the Scroll and Key secret society, a highly exclusive and influential organization at the college. In *James Gamble Rogers and the Architecture of Pragmatism*, Aaron Betsky notes that Gamble was the first in his family to attend an Ivy League school, and the experience seems to have been more cultural than educational. In the new environment, the pursuit of his extracurricular activities seems to have taken precedence over Gamble's academic achievement. During his freshman year, he received some of the lowest grades in the class; in his sophomore year, he received a formal reprimand for low performance.[5]

Rallying himself, Gamble graduated in 1889 and that summer traveled in Europe as part of an exhibition baseball team organized by Albert Goodwill Spalding.[6] Returning from Europe, Gamble took a position in the Chicago architectural firm of Major William LeBaron Jenney (1832–1907), where a Rogers neighbor, William Bryce Mundie, was also employed. Jenney, a former chief engineer during the Civil War, moved to Chicago in 1867 and organized an architectural office that benefited from the city's building boom following the disastrous fire of 1871. Jenney's office, later known as Jenney and Mundie, trained many of Chicago's most important architects, including Daniel H. Burnham, Louis Sullivan, and William Holabird. Jenney has been referred to as the founder of the Chicago School of architecture, primarily because of the firm's pioneering use of iron and steel construction in commercial buildings, which resulted in the creation of the American skyscraper.[7]

Gamble spent less than two years with Jenney's firm, where he learned lessons he said served him throughout his career, including "sensible methods and good, sound construction." Betsky points out that the work in Jenney's office rounded out Gamble's experiences at Yale: "Whereas Rogers had learned about baseball, culture, and social graces at Yale, in Jenney's office he was exposed to the business of architecture."[8]

In 1891 Rogers left the Jenney firm for the firm of Burnham and Root, created in 1873 by Daniel H. Burnham (1846–1912) and John Wellborn Root (1850–1891). Although the firm designed a variety of buildings,

Plate 1. James Gamble Rogers I, ca. 1890. Cabinet photograph, negative CHi-36159. Gift of John J. Glessner Estate. By permission of Chicago Historical Society.

including schools, churches, houses, and railroad stations, its greatest achievements were its tall office buildings. Upon his arrival, Rogers was assigned as superintendent of building for the Ashland Block, located at the northeast corner of Clark and Randolph Streets (destroyed in 1949 for the Union Bus Terminal). As with the other nascent skyscrapers of the time, the sixteen-story building was a brick, terra cotta, and glass envelope around a steel and iron frame.

In less than a year, Rogers left Burnham and Root. He and his younger brother, John Arthur Rogers, operated their own architectural office until the summer of 1892. The brothers completed at least one design together—the Lees Building (demolished 1969), a steel-framed terra cotta and brick office building clearly derived from the early Chicago School teachings Rogers had learned in Jenney's office and with Burnham and Root.

In 1892 Rogers left Chicago to pursue studies in architecture at the École des Beaux-Arts in Paris. As Betsky observes, the summer of 1892 seems an inopportune moment for an aspiring architect to have left Chicago, since the city was on the eve of its grand 1893 World's Columbian Exposition.[9] However, as Betsky suggests, because Rogers lacked formal education in the organizing principles of architecture, he probably felt that the experience would round out his qualifications for continued success in the field he had chosen as his profession.[10]

In the fall of 1898, Rogers was granted a par excellence diploma with medals in both architecture and construction.[11] The École introduced Rogers to the formal organizations of architectural design, as well as to the correct and appropriate uses of historical styles and "orders" of architecture. Upon his return to Chicago, Gamble once again joined his brother, John Arthur, who had maintained the architectural office while Gamble was in Paris. During Gamble's absence, John Arthur had completed a thirteen-story addition to Burnham's Ashland Block, among other projects.[12]

Upon Gamble's return, the office's work revolved around residential designs, which were executed in numerous styles, including Tudor Revival, Arts and Crafts, and even more modern adaptations exhibited by the Chicago School. Rogers returned to historical styles as his primary expression, but unlike architects such as Ralph Adams Cram, who saw the choice of an architectural style as an ideological statement, Rogers selected styles based primarily on what was pleasing and what would work at the site. As will be discussed later, attention to contextual design and this "pragmatic" approach, as Betsky has termed it, was an attribute also found in James Gamble Rogers II's work in Florida.

In 1901 Rogers married Anne Tift Day, whose father was the second president of the Chicago Stock Exchange. Anne's familial connections to the wealthiest of Chicago's residents resulted in several of Rogers' commissions for large mansions.[13]

During this time Rogers was an active member of the Chicago Architectural Club. In 1901 he and non–club member Frank Lloyd Wright judged the club's competition "A United States Embassy in a European Capital."[14] While Rogers and Wright were of different minds concerning the correct direction for modern American architecture, they were both involved in a very exciting and artistically charged environment in Chicago. They were both also interested in advancing their careers through the connections made through the architectural club, as well as through club exhibitions showing their work. Both men ultimately influenced American architecture, though in different styles and in different ways. Wright would have particularly taken issue with Rogers' use of the Gothic style, which, in his opinion, met the needs and conditions of the twelfth century, but did not meet the needs of twentieth-century America. Wright admired the spirit of the Gothic, but did not advocate for a Gothic revival or the use of Neo-Gothic elements. Rogers, on the other hand, was compelled to use historical forms and styles in part because of the context of his buildings, in part because of the desires of his clients, and in part because he found the styles aesthetically pleasing. Wright wanted, and created, a new form of architecture that rejected such historical precedents.

In 1906 Rogers once again made a dramatic professional choice—he moved his office to New York City.[15] Rogers' initial work in New York was commissioned by Edward S. Harkness, who was a member of Yale's class of 1897 and who would play a significant role in Rogers' future career. Between 1908 and 1909 Edward and his half-brother, Charles, both commissioned Fifth Avenue mansions from Rogers. During the first years of his New York practice, Rogers was partnered with Herbert D. Hale (1866–1909), originally of Boston and a graduate of the École des Beaux-Arts. Hale and Rogers' public projects together were the Shelby County Courthouse (1909) and the Central Bank and Trust Building (1910), both in Memphis, Tennessee. Hale retired from the firm in 1907 because of declining health, and he died in 1909, at the age of forty-three.[16]

Between 1907 and 1923 Rogers worked without associates; he then formed James Gamble Rogers, Inc., maintaining the office in New York City until 1947. The Chicago office was closed in 1915, when Gamble's brother relocated to Florida. The work Gamble pursued on the East Coast led to his reputation as an architect of collegiate Neo-Gothic and Neo-Georgian designs. Foremost among his accomplishments are his designs for his alma mater, Yale University. The earliest of these commissions, the Harkness Memorial Quadrangle, which included the Memorial Tower and Gate (1921), was financed by Edward S. Harkness (pl. 2).[17] In his work for Yale, executed throughout the 1920s and 1930s, Rogers perfected his use of historical styles within a collegiate context. In addition to the Harkness Quadrangle (now known as Saybrook and Branford Colleges), Rogers completed six of Yale's other colleges (a total of eight of the first ten established at the school), six fraternities (1927–1932), the Sterling Memorial Library (1931), the Sterling Law School (1931), and the Hall of Graduate Studies (1932). Rogers also completed collegiate designs for Sophie Newcomb College at Tulane University in New Orleans (1918), the Alexander McKinlock Memorial Campus at Northwestern University in Chicago (1926–1927, 1932, 1940), Atlanta College (now Clark-Atlanta University, 1932–1933), and the Harkness Chapel at the Connecticut College for Women (now Connecticut College) in New London, among others.[18] Rogers' firm also completed cam-

Plate 2. Harkness Tower, Yale University. By permission of Michael Marsland/ Yale University.

pus-style designs for the Southern Baptist Theological Seminary in Louisville, Kentucky, as well as several corporate headquarters and large hospital complexes.

From 1923 to 1926 Rogers' work was published in the Chicago Architectural Exhibition League Annual Exhibition Catalogue. In 1923 his Neo-Gothic-style designs for the McKinlock Campus at Northwestern University were displayed, showing massive, fortress-like Neo-Gothic-style educational buildings rising above the smaller-scale dormitories. In 1924 Rogers' medieval-style chapel interiors for Western Theological Seminary in Evanston, Illinois, were shown along with a photograph of the wood and iron gates Rogers designed for the Harkness Memorial Quadrangle at Yale.[19] In 1926 he exhibited his plot plan for the Aetna Life Insurance Company in Hartford, Connecticut. The company's new home office, executed in a Neo-Colonial style, resembled a collegiate plan with interior courtyards arranged in highly formal designs. Rogers' corporate campus focused on a tall central pavilion anchoring a U-shaped complex, which opened onto a baseball diamond with tennis courts beyond. Rogers' choice of exhibition work for his Chicago audience was intended to display not only his range of styles, but also his range of clients, from the collegiate to the corporate, and probably to make sure the midwesterners knew that Rogers could make it, and was making it, in the elite circles of the East Coast.

With the outbreak of World War II, Rogers' work was limited to smaller designs, houses, health care centers, and small hospitals. In the 1930s Rogers had associated with Henry C. Pelton, a noted hospital architect, and subsequently absorbed Pelton's firm into his own.[20] James Gamble Rogers I died in 1947. His son, Francis D. Rogers, continued the architectural firm as Rogers and Butler, in partnership with Jonathan F. Butler.[21] James Gamble Rogers III, FAIA, is a principal in the firm, which is now known as Butler Rogers Baskett Architects, with offices in New York City and South Norwalk, Connecticut.

John Arthur Rogers (1870–1934)

John Arthur Rogers, brother to James Gamble Rogers I and father of James Gamble Rogers II, was born on April 12, 1870, in Louisville, Kentucky, but as noted above, the family moved to Chicago soon afterwards. John Arthur completed four years of study at Northwestern University's Preparatory School (1886–1890), where he was enrolled in the school's scientific curriculum.[22] He then completed a course of study in architecture at MIT (1893). According to MIT records, however, the younger Rogers was not awarded a degree.[23]

As noted earlier, John Arthur was associated with his brother's Chicago architectural office during the early 1890s and maintained the office while his brother attended the École des Beaux-Arts. His involvement may have been periodic, since he would have been engaged in his MIT studies during this time. In 1894 John Arthur took a position with the firm of Joseph Lyman Silsbee (1845–1913), which had employed another young rising architect, Frank Lloyd Wright, just a few years earlier. It may have been that the Rogers office simply did not provide enough work in the older sibling's absence, so John Arthur sought additional employment. Silsbee was a graduate of MIT, which may have served as Rogers' entrée, and had established his Chicago firm in 1882. Silsbee's designs, mostly residential, exhibited a wide array of styles, including Queen Anne, Richardsonian Romanesque, and Colonial Revival. His firm also designed two state buildings at the World's Columbian Exposition held in Chicago in 1893, as well as the "moving sidewalk" used at the fair.[24]

After a short time with Silsbee, John Arthur took a position with the firm of Jenney and Mundie, which earlier had employed his brother. In 1898 James Gamble Rogers I returned from Paris, and he and John Arthur once again operated an architectural office together. As his brother's commissions grew and his interests and office shifted from the Midwest to the East Coast, John Arthur became principal of his own firm, known as "Rogers and Philips" and, later, "Rogers, Philips, and Woodyatt." During this time John Arthur's firm produced several residential designs, schools, and libraries in the Chicago area, while continuing to work on some of Gamble's Chicago projects.[25]

In September 1899 John Arthur Rogers entered into another important partnership—he married Elizabeth Hart Baird, daughter of Lyman Baird and Elizabeth Mather Warner of Chicago. The couple had three children: James Gamble Rogers II (named after John Arthur's older brother), Elizabeth Warner ("Betty"), and Lyman Baird. The latter two children were born in Wilmette, the north Chicago suburb where the couple moved during 1901.

In 1905, the same year James Gamble Rogers I left Chicago for New York City, Philips withdrew from the architectural firm headed by John Arthur. The firm continued as Rogers and Woodyatt until 1913. In that year John Arthur, then only forty-three years old, suffered a serious heart attack. Doctors gave him only six months to live, suggesting that if he were to move to a warmer climate, he might increase his life span by a couple of years.

Heeding their advice, Rogers and his wife moved to Seabreeze, Florida, where his father, Joseph Martin Rogers, had retired years earlier. The three children stayed with their Grandmother Baird back in Winnetka. For the next year or so, John Arthur spent his winters in Florida, where he had started an architectural practice in Daytona Beach. He returned north in the summers, where the family had a second home in Long Lake, Illinois.

In 1915 the entire John Arthur Rogers family moved to Florida. Gamble Rogers II recalled the arduous move made over the early-twentieth-century roadways: "In 1915 we all piled into a Model T Ford and drove to Florida. We took two weeks to do it and the roads were so bad that I remember around Huntsville, Alabama—you had to come through there in those days—the roads were so bad with big rocks and holes and washouts and everything, that my sister and younger brother got out of the car and Mother and Father got out of the car and walked, and I drove it by myself part of the way and they walked a mile or two. That was bad, but we came."[26]

The family first lived in a rented house in Daytona Beach, at the southwest corner of Silver Beach Avenue and Peninsula Drive, but later moved to South Ridgewood Avenue, across from property that would later be developed as the Daytona Golf and Country Club.

At the time, Daytona Beach was a growing tourist destination with active boosters who promoted it as "the most wonderful beautiful beach in the world."[27] The city, incorporated in 1876, had its beginning in the late nineteenth century, when a bridge was constructed across the Halifax River, connecting the mainland with the oceanside peninsula, and Henry Flagler's Florida East Coast Railway pushed southward through the community. Like other seaside resorts, Daytona had several wooden frame hotels and boarding houses that were rented seasonally. Drawn by state boosters, increased accessibility, and the lure of the healthful tonic of the climate, more year-round citizens settled in the area during the 1910s and 1920s. Increased construction of schools, churches, clubs, and other organizations resulted. Most building, however, was interrupted in 1917 by the United States' entry into World War I.

John Arthur Rogers, though infirmed by his heart condition, volunteered to serve his country during the conflict. Taking advantage of his seamanship rather than his architectural abilities, the navy saw fit to assign Ensign Rogers to the Port Guards in Key West (pl. 3). From April 4, 1917, to January 2, 1918, he was responsible for onboard searches of vessels seeking entry into U.S.-controlled waters. According to Gamble, his father's main vessel during this period was the U.S.S. *Anton Dohrn*, a 71-foot motorboat constructed in Miami in 1911. The vessel, commissioned in October 1917, was leased by the navy for one dollar and was returned to her owner after the armistice. According to Gamble, the boat was owned by multimillionaire and philanthropist Andrew Carnegie.[28]

After his service in Key West, Rogers returned to his home and practice in Daytona Beach. During the late 1910s and into the 1920s, Daytona and the surrounding area, like much of Florida, experienced an increase in tourism, which led to an increase in its year-round population. During the war years wealthy northerners, no longer able to travel abroad because of the hostilities, turned their attention southward, coaxed by developers who followed the earlier efforts of Henry Flagler, who died in 1913.

Plate 3. John Arthur Rogers,
ca. 1912. Courtesy of RLF.

John Arthur Rogers' architectural practice included projects of nearly every building type during this period. A small but thriving group of architects was practicing in the beachfront community at the time, producing architecturally conservative but well-executed designs. Some of the architects practicing in Daytona during the 1920s included Elias DeLaHaye, Jacob Espedahl, C. E. Garnett, and Harry M. Griffin. The majority of Rogers' projects were residential designs (estimated at nearly 100) for some of Daytona's prominent citizens, including T. J. McReynolds Sr., executive vice president of the Atlantic Bank and Trust Co., and C. M. Bray.[29] He also produced civic designs, such as the Peninsula Club (1922; Goodall Avenue and South Peninsula Drive) and a clubhouse for the Daytona Golf and Country Club (ca. 1925; South Ridgewood Avenue), which was Daytona's first country club, to which many of Daytona's prominent citizens belonged. His commercial projects included the Osceola-Gramatan Inn, a hotel formerly located on South Ridgewood Avenue.

In addition to his social memberships, Rogers also was involved in the civic life of Daytona Beach. From 1924 to 1925, he served on the city council for Daytona. He also served as secretary of the local Red Cross for three years and was the first post commander of the Daytona American Legion.[30]

Two other pursuits occupied John Arthur's time: sailing and art. As mentioned earlier, Rogers' boating ability was one of the reasons he was sent to Key West during the war. Having lived in Chicago by Lake Michigan, the Rogers family seems for generations to have been drawn to the water. Joseph Martin Rogers wintered on the seashore in Seabreeze; for several years John Arthur had a summer house on Long Lake, northwest of Chicago; and James Gamble Rogers I had a summer home in Black Point, Connecticut, a summer resort area he founded near Niantic on a peninsula that stretches into Long Island Sound.[31] All appear to have been able seamen. John Arthur was a member of the Halifax River Yacht Club, whose former clubhouse still stands in downtown Daytona near the Orange Avenue bridge. Later, he served as commodore of the Allandale Yacht Club.

John Arthur was also a talented artist, working in wood etchings. In 1932 his interests in the arts led him to found, along with local Daytona painter Don J. Emery, the Daytona Art League. The League, now know as the Art League of Daytona Beach, was dedicated to "the encouragement and promotion of all the graphic and plastic arts."[32] Rogers was the League's first president, and after his death in 1934, his wife, Elizabeth, became president.

Around 1926 Rogers built a home in Allandale, along the Halifax River just south of Daytona. Heeding his doctor's advice, Rogers had moved south to improve his health, hopefully for a couple years. As it turned out, he lived for another twenty years. He died at his home in 1934, leaving behind a professional legacy, as well as a civic and social one. His son, James Gamble Rogers II, who worked in his father's architectural office, would continue in his father's field, and would provide Central Florida with some of its most notable buildings.

James Gamble Rogers II (1901–1990)

James Gamble Rogers II, son of Elizabeth Baird and John Arthur Rogers, was born on January 24, 1901, in Chicago and lived with his family in the northern suburb of Winnetka until he was a teenager. Because of his father's failing health, the family left Chicago in 1915 for Daytona Beach, Florida. Having completed his first two years of high school at New Trier High School in Kenilworth, Illinois, Gamble enrolled as a junior in Daytona Beach High School, where he participated in a number of extracurricular and social activities. Displaying an array of artistic talents, Gamble illustrated the cover of his senior class yearbook, the 1918 *Sentinel*, with a wood etching of a sailboat on open water, with a palm tree in the foreground. As art director for the *Sentinel* staff, he also provided etchings for each section of the yearbook. He was a manager for the basketball team, earning the respect of his teammates and an honorary varsity letter, and served as treasurer for the athletic association. In the latter role, Gamble was responsible for writing and circulating a petition among local businesspeople to support the high school's athletics (a precursor to today's booster clubs). In its first year, the association collected $158.00. Gamble was also the president of the Areopagus literary society, which was named for the sacred hill in ancient Athens. Demonstrating his literary skill, Gamble published his "Ode to Daybreak" in the yearbook, describing the poet's dream of paddling across the ocean in the moonlight. Gamble's dreams were also the topic of the senior class forecast, which humorously depicted class members in the far-off year of 1950: "I see Gamble Rogers and Richard Wipple, the two greatest draughtsmen of their day. It was their plans that made practical the New York–London bridge."[33]

Gamble's drafting plans, however, were put on hold immediately following his graduation from Daytona Beach High School. He had contacted Dartmouth College concerning admission, but the college informed Gamble that they did not have room for him in their upcoming class and that it would be two or three years before they could admit him. They also requested more information on Gamble's high school, which they had never heard of, and asked for proof of the school's accreditation.[34] Gamble was successful in gaining accreditation for the high school, and for the next three years he worked at Daytona's Merchants Bank. He started as a bookkeeper, then was promoted to a teller, and finally was placed in charge of the safe-deposit vault.[35] His positions indicate that he was seen as a trustworthy individual who possessed mathematical as well as interpersonal skills.

In 1921 Gamble entered Dartmouth, attending on a swimming scholarship. According to John Hopewell Rogers, Gamble's son, his father most likely chose Dartmouth, rather than his father's MIT or his uncle's Yale, because his friend Dan Leonard from Winnetka was attending Dartmouth.[36] The financial incentive of a scholarship probably aided in his selection.

Like his uncle, Gamble seems to have enjoyed the variety of opportunities presented to him in the invigorating atmosphere of college and quickly became a star athlete. His first season at Dartmouth was only

Plate 4. James Gamble Rogers II as a student at Dartmouth College (1923 or 1924). Courtesy of RLF.

the second year that swimming had been recognized as a team sport at the college. Gamble swam the 100-yard breaststroke, in which he broke intercollegiate time records and continually placed in meets; he twice won the New England Intercollegiate Breaststroke Championship (1922 and 1923). During his tenure at Dartmouth, Gamble also won an All-American citation and qualified for the 1924 U.S. Olympic swim team. In 1924 he was named captain of the Dartmouth team. Gamble also was a member of the Tau chapter of Phi Sigma Kappa fraternity and a member of the tennis team.[37]

Academically, Gamble took the largest number of semester hours in Spanish, history, and mathematics. He earned his best grades in English and Spanish classes.

Gamble's athletic and educational ambitions, however, came to a halt during his third (junior) year at Dartmouth. In 1924 he withdrew from college after his father suffered another serious heart attack. Returning to Daytona, the younger Rogers assumed a place in his father's architectural firm, where for the next ten years he gained professional experience and took on responsibilities for architectural projects. Ini-

Plate 5. The 1924 Dartmouth College swimming team. Rogers is seated in the center of the front row. From the 1925 Aegis, Dartmouth yearbook. Courtesy of Archives Department, Dartmouth College Library.

Plate 6. James Gamble Rogers II as captain of the Dartmouth College swimming team. Courtesy of Archives Department, Dartmouth College Library.

tially, Gamble used his artistic talent in the office and served as a draftsman. His knowledge of construction then led him into the roles of structural designer and construction supervisor. He also continued his formal education through the American Correspondence School (of Chicago), with courses in mechanical engineering and architecture.

After several years of observation and practical application, Gamble became the office's building designer. It was during these ten years in his father's office that Gamble developed his ability to manage people and projects, to solve problems creatively, and to produce architectural designs that satisfied his clients' needs, budgets, and desire for social status.

With no formal architectural degree, Rogers relied on the licensed architects in his father's office to review and correct his drawings. His father signed much of his early work, and associate architects, such as David B. Hyer or George Camp Keiser in Winter Park, often signed other drawings.

In 1928 Gamble opened a branch of his father's office in the developing community of Winter Park, located approximately an hour inland from the east coast of Florida. Gamble said he liked the people in Winter Park, many of whom had Chicago ties, and that he thought of it as "an awfully nice place to live." He had first visited Winter Park back in 1917, when an uncle, his mother's brother whose fiancée's family wintered in Florida, was married in the All Saints Episcopal Church there.[38]

The friendships Gamble was developing in Winter Park would serve him well during the next few years. At a beach party in Daytona, he met Evelyn Claire Smith of Atlanta. Evelyn, born on January 15, 1902, was a graduate of Agnes Scott College in Atlanta. Over the next few years, Gamble courted Evelyn, whom he called "Red," often traveling to see her in Georgia. The couple married on September 28, 1929, and enjoyed sixty years together.

Through a creative business deal, Gamble secured a building lot on Winter Park's Woo Island, also known as Bear Island and now known as the Isle of Sicily, located on Lake Maitland. By January 1, 1930, just four months after his marriage, Rogers had designed and built Four Winds, a romantic cottage in the French Provincial style, for Evelyn and himself. The completion of this house drew much admiration locally and nationally, through publication in architectural magazines.

In 1934 Rogers sat for the State of Florida's licensing exam. John Hopewell Rogers recalls his father's frustration with taking the test, a portion of which consisted of a large design problem wherein the intern

Plate 7. Evelyn Claire Smith (left front) and James Gamble Rogers II (right front) at their engagement party aboard Bob and May Arrell's boat in Daytona Beach (1928). Courtesy of RLF.

was required to fully develop a project in detailed plans, sections, and elevations. Gamble developed a hotel with a central atrium, an element commonly found in hotels today. The Florida Board of Architecture, however, rejected the solution, saying the atrium element was far too impractical.[39] Gamble successfully passed the Florida exam in 1935 and received license number 124 from the National Council of Architectural Registration Boards. Later, he also was registered in Illinois, New York, and Georgia.

In 1934, after twenty years in Florida, John Arthur Rogers died at his home in Allandale. After his father's death Gamble closed his father's Daytona Beach architectural office and moved to Winter Park. He mulled over going back to Chicago, but decided that the Florida climate suited him best. While he continued to produce designs for clients on the east coast of Florida, it appears that Gamble was drawn to the intellectual, cultural, and social life that was thriving in Winter Park.

At first, Gamble allied himself with local architect David B. Hyer. In November 1935 Hyer moved to Charleston, South Carolina, and closed his Winter Park office. That year Gamble opened his own firm. Rogers' influence over Winter Park's architecture was under way.

2

Beginning in Winter Park

THE WINTER PARK that lured Gamble from his family's oceanside home had been evolving for more than forty years. The town's modern-day history can be traced back to Loring Chase, a real estate developer from Chicago, who suffered from bronchitis and came to Florida on the advice of his doctor. In 1881 Chase visited a friend in Orlando, who drove his guest around the nearby chain of Lakes Virginia, Osceola, and Maitland. Sensing that the area had development potential, Chase and his partner, Oliver E. Chapman, purchased 600 acres and platted a town.[1]

Chase embarked on a program of boosterism and entrepreneurship to lure northern vacationers further south and inland from the traditional Florida destinations of Jacksonville and St. Augustine to Winter Park. While a small community known as Osceola already existed near the lakes, Chase began a building campaign in 1882 that included a train depot, which was serviced by a branch of Henry Plant's South Florida Railroad; a general store and post office; and the Rogers House, a hotel on the shores of Lake Virginia, the owners and operators of which were of no relation to the architect. Photographic images of 1880s Winter Park show largely uninhabited sand streets with stands of tall pine trees and a few buildings dotting the landscape, all of which must have made Chase's job of selling tourism harder as compared with the elaborate hotels and facilities in Flagler's St. Augustine and in Jacksonville (pl. 8).

In 1884 Winter Park was selected as the site for a new college supported by the Congregational Church. The town had stiff competition from five other Central Florida communities vying for the privilege, and economic boon, of hosting the college. Once again, it was a Chicago businessman who secured Winter Park's future. Alonzo Rollins, for whom the college was named, donated $50,000 to the town's effort in attracting the school. Rollins College was incorporated on April 28, 1885.

Chapman sold his interests in his Winter Park holdings to Chase in 1885, and soon the Winter Park Improvement Association (later known

Plate 8. Park Avenue, looking east, ca. 1888. By permission of Florida State Archives, Tallahassee.

as the Chamber of Commerce) was organized and chartered by the state to promote the town.[2] While primarily serving as a winter refuge from northern winters, Winter Park developed into a citrus region, with orange and grapefruit trees covering much of the acreage in town.

By 1890 Winter Park boasted a population of 600. Seasonal residents often stayed in one of the new hotels built especially to accommodate the winter tourists. The earliest inn was originally known as the Rogers House, which opened in 1882 with thirty rooms and a locally famous dining room. The three-story frame structure, located at the intersection of Morse and Interlachen Avenues, featured several porches and a large portico on each end of the building. A new owner renamed the hotel the Virginia Inn, which was the name it operated under until 1966. The "old" Seminole Hotel, built by Henry Plant in 1886 and located on Lake Osceola, was a 150-room resort—at the time the largest hotel in the state. In its first year, the Seminole hosted 2,300 guests and as a luxury resort offered such activities as "croquet, tennis, billiards, and bowling; horses and buggies; fishing and boating in the chain of lakes; and musical entertainment."[3] The hotel burned in 1902, and a "new" Seminole Hotel opened in 1913 on Lake Osceola at Webster Avenue. The new Seminole served vacationers to the area for more than fifty years. The Hotel Alabama, built in 1922 and containing eighty rooms, is the last of Winter Park's residential hotels still extant. Located on the

Plate 9. The "old" Seminole Hotel, 1896. By permission of Florida State Archives, Tallahassee.

Figure 1. Map of Winter Park, 1888. By permission of Department of College Archives and Special Collections, Olin Library, Rollins College, Winter Park, Florida.

southeastern shore of Lake Maitland, the hotel was converted into con-
dominiums in the late 1970s, but retains its appearance of an early-
twentieth-century hotel, with a large lawn and tropical gardens.

One of the most notable examples of Winter Park's late-nineteenth-
century private residential architecture is the Comstock house, or
Eastbank, located on Bonita Drive on the eastern shore of Lake Osceola.
In 1883 William C. Comstock, the former president of the Chicago
Board of Trade, built this impressive shingle-clad Queen Anne structure
around an earlier frame farmhouse. In 1898 Edward Hill Brewer constructed The Palms, as a winter cottage along Lake Osceola. The house,
purported to be a replica of the family's Cortland, New York, residence,
was a large three-story frame Queen Anne–style dwelling with projecting gable bays, a wraparound porch, and a widow's walk. In the 1920s
Brewer decided to renovate the 21-room house in the Colonial Revival
style, which we see today. These and other frame residences, some modest and some quite large, began to develop along the shores of Winter
Park's chain of lakes (fig. 1).

In less than a decade Chase's dream of building a town seemed to
have taken root. The dream, though, was threatened in 1895, when a
killing freeze wiped out nearly all of the groves in the area, financially
devastating many of the residents. Undeterred, many people stayed and
replanted the citrus, along with other crops. W. C. Temple, for whom
the Temple orange was named and whose property was located between
Palmer Avenue and Lake Maitland, embarked on a distinguished career
as a grove owner and general manager of the Florida Citrus Exchange,
which he helped to establish.

In 1923 the town of Winter Park was incorporated as a city, having reached the requisite number of residents. Numerous hotels, commercial enterprises, and residences had been built in the ensuing years.
A college, public library, woman's club, and chamber of commerce
rounded out the list of intellectual and social organizations that flour-
ished in the new city.

It was during the first years of the twentieth century that many of
Winter Park's most famous residents made the place their home, if only
seasonally. In 1904 Charles Hosmer Morse, another Chicagoan, purchased hundreds of acres in Winter Park, effectively buying out Chase
and Chapman's original plat. Morse's home, known as Osceola Lodge,
was typical of the houses found in Winter Park during this time in that
it was of frame construction clad with clapboards, fronted with a large

porch, and, in style, was similar to Victorian-era dwellings in other communities throughout the country.

Commercial structures in the town and even the institutional buildings at Rollins College were likewise of frame construction and were variously decorated with Queen Anne or Italianate details. In the 1920s, however, few examples of the Spanish style of architecture could be found in Winter Park.[4] The Woman's Club, for instance, constructed in 1921 and located on Interlachen Avenue, exhibited a Classical Revival image, with a colonnade across its front facade. The design of the University Club, constructed on Webster Avenue in 1921, was a rare example of the use of Spanish design for public buildings. The one-story stucco building featured a triple-arched entry porch and a low-slung hipped roof covered with wooden shingles.

It was into this atmosphere that Gamble Rogers entered in 1928, when he opened a branch of his father's architectural office in Winter Park. The decade between 1920 and 1930 was one of great economic and social growth, during which the city's population grew to 5,200 permanent residents. With Hamilton Holt as its new president, Rollins College was entering into its most prosperous period yet. Holt, whose tenure at the school lasted twenty-five years, until his retirement in 1949, was responsible for renovating both the college's curriculum and its architectural image, which was transformed from a collection of frame cottages into an attractive campus of Mediterranean-style buildings.

Although Rogers had completed several residential designs in the Daytona Beach area and in Fern Park and Casselberry, two small communities north of Winter Park, he had completed only one residential design in Winter Park, for William B. Follett. Soon, however, Rogers' role as an image maker for the Central Florida region would begin in earnest.

Four Winds

During the late 1920s and early 1930s, Rogers was completing mostly modest but notable residential designs under the banner of his father's firm. What we see in these designs is Rogers' preference for expressed structural members used in romantic, rustic styles. The house completed in 1928 for real estate agent Victor N. Camp in Ormond Beach is a particularly intriguing example of Rogers' early use of elements of the

Plate 10. Victor N. Camp House, Ormond Beach, 1928. Photograph by Victor N. Camp. Courtesy of RLF.

French Provincial style to create a pleasing and romantic domestic environment. The house was featured in *House Beautiful* as part of the portfolio of houses submitted to the magazine's 1929 Small House Competition.[5] Though it did not win an award, it was interesting enough to the editors to offer it as an admirable design, and Rogers received a small honorarium. It was also the only design by a Florida architect to be published in the competition, which was dominated by designs from the East Coast, New England, and California. The two-story frame Camp house was covered with a light buff-colored stucco finish. A cross-gable roof of weathered wooden shingles covered the T-shaped plan. Punched openings with no surrounds held multipaned cypress casement windows. A curving stone path led to the arched door opening on the front, which was flanked by a shapely, stucco-clad exterior chimney. The sloping nature of the site gave the design a stepped appearance and allowed for the creation of a stone patio and a pool in the back.

The plan of the Camp house was practical and efficient. One entered the house at the end of a small hall at the edge of a large living room. The projecting cross-gable area in the front held the kitchen, breakfast nook, and pantry on the first floor and a closet and storage area on the second floor. Two bedrooms and a bath were located on each floor. Rogers tucked the stairway into the back corner of the living room, a placement commonly seen in Colonial-era dwellings. In this way, the stairs did not intrude upon any living space, and the area below was utilized for closets. The plan of the Camp house reflects contemporary tendencies, as

Plate 11. Fern Park Post Office Building, ca. 1930. Courtesy of RLF.

noted by the accompanying magazine article, to jettison the formal dining room completely. Instead, a breakfast alcove was provided, and a dining area was informally set up within the living room.

While the Camp house lacked applied decoration, we can already see Rogers' interest in the French Provincial style in his use of stucco-clad exterior walls, punched openings with casement windows, and a steeply pitched gable roof covered with wooden shakes. Later, the architect would refine his use of these elements in his own home.

During the late 1920s Rogers also completed several residential projects in the small community of Fern Park, located in Seminole County just north of Winter Park. Hibbard Casselberry developed the area as a retirement community, and the town took its name from the fern farms, or ferneries, that operated there. Residents were each provided with an acre of land on which a wood-frame fernery was built, equipped, and planted by the marketing association. Residents were responsible for building their own homes, but plans were often suggested. The retirees were "assured income for life" through the year-round harvesting of the ferns, which were sold through the marketing association.[6]

Rogers designed an office for the ferneries' operation, as well as several small French Provincial–style dwellings for some of the local residents and the local post office. Though all the houses have been demolished, photographs and drawings of some of them remain. In 1931

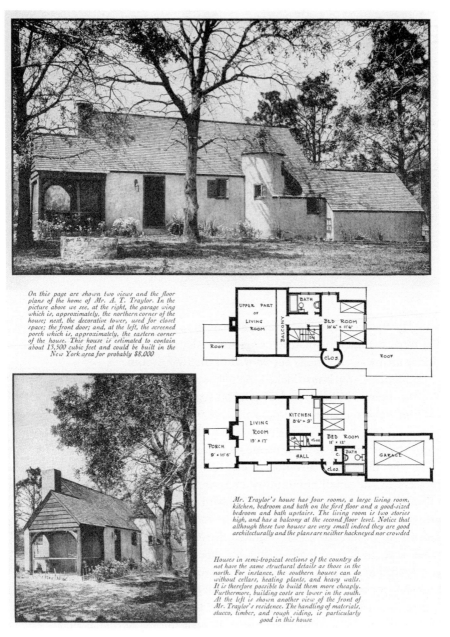

On this page are shown two views and the floor plans of the home of Mr. A. T. Traylor. In the picture above we see, at the right, the garage wing which is, approximately, the northern corner of the house; next, the decorative tower, used for closet space; the front door; and, at the left, the screened porch which is, approximately, the eastern corner of the house. This house is estimated to contain about 13,500 cubic feet and could be built in the New York area for probably $8,000

Mr. Traylor's house has four rooms, a large living room, kitchen, bedroom and bath on the first floor and a good-sized bedroom and bath upstairs. The living room is two stories high, and has a balcony at the second floor level. Notice that although these two houses are very small indeed they are good architecturally and the plans are neither hackneyed nor crowded

Houses in semi-tropical sections of the country do not have the same structural details as those in the north. For instance, the southern houses can do without cellars, heating plants, and heavy walls. It is therefore possible to build them more cheaply. Furthermore, building costs are lower in the south. At the left is shown another view of the front of Mr. Traylor's residence. The handling of materials, stucco, timber, and rough siding, is particularly good in this house

Plate 12. Advertisement for A. T. Traylor house in Fern Park, Florida, 1930. From American Home magazine.

Plate 13. James Gamble Rogers II house on Isle of Sicily, Winter Park, Florida, 1930. Courtesy of RLF.

Rogers' designs for the small French Provincial A. T. Traylor cottage and a home for Mrs. Helena K. Smith were advertised in *American Home* magazine. Since Fern Park was such a small development, it may be that Rogers, per Casselberry's request, was seeking to unify the appearances of the buildings to give the area a recognizable architectural identity. Rogers' buildings were similar in that they had stucco walls and featured exposed structural members painted or stained a dark brown. Materials applied between these members included rough stucco and brick laid in a herringbone pattern. Small punched openings held multipaned casement windows, and the houses were covered by steep gable roofs clad with wooden shingles.

In 1928 several Winter Park businessmen purchased Bear (or Woo) Island, now known as the Isle of Sicily, located in Lake Maitland, and were interested in platting lots and developing new houses. Rogers agreed to help in the development if the company would in turn give him his choice of the lots on which to build his own home. The next year, construction began on Rogers' Four Winds, which was designed in the style of a French country home.

Locally, the house was greatly admired and drew visitors from throughout Winter Park. The house was also featured in seven different architectural magazines over the next few years, bringing it national attention. Although the house did not produce immediate success for the new island development, it did bolster the architect's practice.

Rogers recounted that he received the commission for Robert Bruce Barbour's house based solely on Barbour's admiration of Four Winds.[7]

Rogers received another publicity boost when several of his houses were photographed by New York photographer Harold Haliday Costain. Beginning in the late 1920s, Costain made three or four trips a year to Florida on assignment for different magazines. He had spent some time as a still photographer for a movie company, but when the movie industry moved west to Hollywood, Costain stayed in the East.[8] One magazine Costain worked for on a regular basis was *American Home*, for which he photographed the Traylor cottage and other ferneries buildings. Costain also photographed Rogers' houses built for the Barbours, the Ingrams, and the McAllasters, and captured their exotic architecture in his evocative black-and-white prints. Exhibitions of these prints in New York galleries brought Rogers recognition from afar. According to Rogers, the Nobel Prize–winning author Sinclair Lewis had seen the Barbour house in an exhibit in New York, and when he visited Rollins College in the late 1930s, he was eager to see the house. The Barbours held a dinner in Lewis' honor.[9]

Residential commissions multiplied for Rogers as others became acquainted with his work through publications, word of mouth, and personal admiration. During this time of the Great Depression, however, only a few citizens could afford such a luxury as a new house, some of which were only seasonally occupied. Within this elite circle, friends often spread the word about the young architect and his talent. The Shippens, for whom Rogers completed a Spanish-influenced residence in 1931, were friends of the Barbours and encouraged their efforts to engage the architect. The Barbours contracted with the Noyeses, an artistic couple residing in Winter Park, to help decorate their Rogers-designed Andalusian-style home with authentic Spanish furnishings and, in the process, inspired the Noyeses to commission a residence from Rogers.

Like his uncle and father before him, Rogers was expanding his client base through friends with social connections, as well as through his architectural skills. Several of his early relationships had a distinctly Chicago cast to them. Dan Leonard, a schoolmate from Winnetka and later Dartmouth, was among these friends. Rogers completed house designs for Leonard's uncle, Edgar C. Leonard, as well as several designs for Leonard's sister and brother-in-law from Winnetka, Mary Elizabeth (Mel) and Hubert (Hibbard) Casselberry Sr., the developer of the Fern Park community. The home of William Follett and his wife, Edna, who were a decade older than Rogers and his group of friends, became an unofficial gathering spot for the younger set, who "gathered at their house every afternoon for drinks and nobody got soused at all, but would sit around and talk." This sort of camaraderie put Rogers "right in the center of the people who would be building the most elegant houses" in Winter Park at the time.[10] Added to these individuals were the professors associated with Rollins College, with whom Rogers would soon become acquainted, including Rhea Smith, originally from Texas and a history professor, and his wife, Dorothy Lockhart, of Philadelphia. The artistic, intellectual, and social climate of Winter Park provided a ripe opportunity for the young architect to help such clients build their dreams.

Winter Park was a small town, and Gamble Rogers was its prized architect. Other architects were practicing, both in Winter Park and in Orlando, but the field remained small. D. Harold Hare, George Camp Keiser, Maurice G. Kressly, Jack Moore, L. A. Hatton, Henry Whitworth, Robert Murphy, George F. Dunham, F. Earl DeLoe, Harry L. Lindsey, and Kenneth Miller were some of the local architects whose work regularly appeared in professional magazines such as *Florida Architecture and Allied Arts* and *Architecturally Winter Park*.[11] These magazines show that a number of styles were popular throughout the state, including Mediterranean-influenced styles, Colonial Revival, and Art Deco and Moderne, though the latter two styles appeared most frequently in Miami rather than other parts of Florida. Local shows, such as exhibits at the Morse Gallery of Art at Rollins College, also presented examples of contemporary Florida architecture and were often accompanied by roundtable discussions and lectures in which Rogers participated regularly.

The period between 1930 and the beginning of World War II was a prolific one for Rogers, during which he created many of his most memorable residential designs in Winter Park. The Andalusian-style Barbour house and the Spanish-influenced Shippen house were completed during this time, as were the Spanish-style Noyes, Holt, and McAllaster houses; the French Provincial Ingram house; the Moderne Jewett house; and the thoroughly Modern Leonard house. A Tudoresque design was completed for the Burress house; a Colonial Revival–style dwelling was designed for U. T. Bradley; and small shingle cottages were completed for Doris Bingham and Grace Edwards. During the decade of the 1930s, Rogers completed more than sixty residential designs or designs for additions or alterations in and around Winter Park.

Rogers' career during the 1930s involved a steady flow of commissions, but, the architect noted later, his work was not all-consuming. Living on Winter Park's chain of lakes, Rogers was able to frequently indulge his love of sailing. With like-minded neighbors, he helped to organize the Winter Park Boat Club, which held its first race on Lake Virginia in February 1934. Given that work was slow during the Depression, Rogers would close his offices early on Wednesday for such races. In the club's inaugural race, Rogers' 12-foot *Jolly Roger* placed first.[12]

During these years Rogers also devoted himself to civic life through participation in several panel discussions on urban planning and civic beautification. He presented a lecture at the Woman's Club of Winter Park, "Architectural Touches for Civic Improvement," and he and fellow architect Harold Hare spoke to the same club to offer propositions to the question "What can be done to make Winter Park more beautiful?" Similar topics were being discussed at civic meetings throughout urban America as cities grew quickly, often with little or no planning. These efforts clearly had their roots in the City Beautiful movement, which began in the late nineteenth century in larger, more urban areas such as New York City, Boston, and Chicago. Women's groups in particular challenged city councils to beautify their cities by addressing such issues as zoning in order to evoke civic loyalty, as well as moral rectitude. In Winter Park, issues such as less obtrusive signage and an increase in street trees were discussed. Hare contributed by writing a zoning law for Winter Park and advising on the employment of a building inspector for new construction.[13]

Professional activities also occupied Rogers during the 1930s, including his membership in the American Institute of Architects (AIA) and his efforts to establish the Mid-Florida chapter. Rogers attended the AIA convention in New Orleans in 1938 as the delegate from the State Board of Architecture, of which he was a member from 1935 to 1946, and served as president of the chapter from 1939 to 1943.

Though Rogers was now fully devoted to architecture as a profession, he continued his pursuit of writing, both formally and informally. In 1935 the *Architectural Forum* published his article on termite control. The problem, one with which any Floridian is familiar, was not well studied at the time and presented owners collectively with an annual $50 million bill. Rogers blamed some of this damage on the construction methods employed in the 1920s building boom, during which "thousands of cheap frame houses were thrown together with no precautionary methods to prevent the termite from flourishing. Many of

Plate 14. The Caprice *and part of her crew in Mayport after surviving the September 1938 hurricane. Pictured are Bob Murdock, George Tuttle, and Hibbard Casselberry. Photograph by James Gamble Rogers II. Courtesy of RLF.*

these houses were stuccoed directly on wood lap, the stucco being brought down to the soil all around the building. Sap lumber was used, there was little or no sub–first floor ventilation, and the result was a perfect working condition for the termite."[14] Rogers' article provided twelve fundamental rules to prevent termite infestation in new construction, as well as repairing termite damage found in existing buildings. Afterwards, he became a consultant to the Forest Products Laboratory in Madison, Wisconsin, and helped the company to correct and update its bulletins on termite control.

Rogers completed another bit of writing in 1938: his account of being caught in the Atlantic Ocean on the 55-foot yacht *Caprice* during the decade's fiercest hurricane. Gamble's Winter Park friends George Tuttle and Bob Murdock had purchased the boat in Fort Lauderdale and decided to sail up to Mayport, near Jacksonville, to bring the yacht into the St. Johns River. Gamble was selected as additional crew, and he brought along his sailing buddy Hibbard Casselberry Sr. The crew set off with a local forecast—all that was available at the time—of fair weather for the next thirty-six hours. Unbeknownst to the crew, a massive hurricane had formed off the African coast on September 10, and it was headed toward the east coast of the United States.

The 300–mile trip to Mayport usually took three days, but this trip would last five. The most intense sustained winds of the unnamed hur-

Plate 15. The Rogers family, ca. 1948, at their home in Temple Grove. Evelyn and Gamble, Jack (left) and Jimmy (right), and Vicky. Courtesy of Archives Department, Dartmouth College Library.

ricane were measured on September 19 and 20 at 140 miles per hour, with an internal barometric pressure of 938 millibars—a category 4 hurricane. Although the storm never made landfall in Florida, the fringes of it racked the *Caprice* and its crew for two days and a night. The story, as written by Rogers, bears similarities to Stephen Crane's "The Open Boat," which is Crane's own account of being shipwrecked by a storm off the coast of Florida. Though never published, Gamble's story is a detailed and thrilling depiction of his terrifying adventure.

In 1941 Gamble and Evelyn, now with two sons, James Gamble IV and John Hopewell, sold their little cottage on the island and purchased the Temple Grove estate, which was located between Lake Osceola and Palmer Avenue. (James Gamble Rogers III was the eldest son of James Gamble Rogers I.) The 17-acre parcel was part of Louis Hake's former citrus grove where the Temple orange—a cross between an orange and a tangerine—was first discovered. The Rogers family initially lived in a Cracker-style frame cottage that was one of three extant buildings on the property. The two-bedroom house, built around 1890, was "painted red with white trim and it was in the center of the property with three large oak trees around it."[15] In 1948 Rogers designed a larger Greek Revival house and sited it south of the small cottage, which was then moved to property just outside the grove (pl. 15). In the 1970s the Rogerses' sons partitioned the estate into a residential development known as Temple Grove. Gamble Rogers retained about three acres around his Greek Revival home, including a large expanse of lawn down to the lakeshore. He lived there until his death in 1990.

Work with Rollins

Rogers' direct involvement with the planning and architecture of Rollins College began in the 1940s, although the architect had watched with admiration as the school erected well-designed Spanish Mediterranean Revival–style buildings during the late 1920s and 1930s. Under the direction of Rollins president Hamilton Holt, the architectural firm of Kiehnel and Elliott from Miami had set the tone for the campus's Spanish architectural theme through numerous designs for dormitories, classroom buildings, and most notably the Annie Russell Theater. Ralph Adams Cram, America's foremost proponent of the Gothic Revival style, added to the Rollins collection with his 1926 design for the Knowles Memorial Chapel, which was expressed in a hybrid Mediterranean style drawing on both Spanish Renaissance and Baroque precedents. Rogers greatly admired Cram's work and often cited the chapel as one of the best buildings in Winter Park.

In 1942, after Kiehnel's death, George Spohn, who had served as an assistant to Kiehnel and Elliott on many of their projects at the school, was selected as campus architect. Spohn was chosen over Rogers, who had submitted his portfolio and resume to the college. While President Holt most likely had a personal inclination to select Rogers, the school apparently felt some sort of allegiance to Spohn, but asked Rogers to assist in completing designs.[16] Through this association, Rogers designed the Mills Memorial Library in 1948. Though Spohn is often credited with the design, the detail and accurateness of the Spanish elements on the building are clearly from Rogers' pencil (pl. 15).

After Spohn's death in the early 1950s, Rogers continued design work for the college for another forty years. From the 1950s through the 1980s, his firm was responsible for the design of four new residence halls and the upgrading of nine others, the Crummer Business School, the Rose Skillman Dining Hall, the Archibald Granville Bush Science Center, and an addition to Cram's Knowles Chapel. Rogers' final design for the school was the Olin Library in 1986, which maintained the Span-

Plate 16. Mills Library, Rollins College. Rendering by Laurance W. Hitt. By permission of Department of College Archives and Special Collections, Olin Library, Rollins College, Winter Park, Florida.

ish vocabulary of the other major buildings at the school. The Florida AIA presented Rogers with its State Craftsmanship Award for the excellence of the stucco moldings and architectural details for the library.

Rogers' professional relationship with members of Rollins' staff and the visibility afforded him through his work at the school led to a number of commissions from faculty members and administrators, including George Holt, admissions director and son of college president Hamilton Holt; Alexander Buel Trowbridge Jr., assistant professor of religion and ethics; Ervin Theodore Brown, college treasurer and business manager; and Udolpho Theodore Bradley, assistant professor of history and government.

Work during World War II

The United States' entry into World War II had a devastating effect on construction projects throughout the country. Not only was it nearly impossible to secure building supplies, which were being funneled into government projects, but manpower was also in short supply as able-bodied men enlisted in the armed services. With much of his work heretofore consisting of private-sector commissions, Rogers decided to suspend active operation in his Winter Park architectural firm for the duration of the war and applied for a civil service appointment. Completing his application on June 9, 1942, Rogers stated that he could begin work by June 24. His preference was for a position writing specifica-

Plate 17. Olin Library, Rollins College. Photograph by author.

tions or cost estimating in the southeastern part of the United States or in the Caribbean.

On July 7, 1942, Rogers was accepted into the civil service, and on August 11 he was assigned as an engineer in the architectural section of the U.S. Engineer Office in Wilmington, North Carolina. This district office of the Corps of Engineers was involved in the design and construction of airfields and air bases and mobilization construction at several southern bases. Prior to World War II the office of the quartermaster general (QM) had been responsible for all military construction, but it quickly became clear that the QM could not provide all necessary designs for the massive wartime buildup. The corps, on the other hand, had "a large construction network already in place and a long history of handling major projects."[17] In November 1940 the War Department transferred responsibility for construction of Army Air Corps facilities to the Corps of Engineers. A little more than a year later, the corps was responsible for all army construction.

Rogers' personnel records show that in his role as a project design–control engineer, he was responsible for coordinating all data, drawings, designs, and specifications for the military projects assigned to his office. Within a year he was promoted to senior engineer level and made assistant chief of the Engineering Division and acting chief of Military Design, which increased his annual pay from $3,800 to $4,600. Reviews of his performance indicate that he possessed a thorough knowledge of architectural engineering, and the ability to plan and supervise large projects. Rogers' work for the corps included designs for airplane hangars and military camp construction. His role included designing and preparing working drawings for camp buildings, modifying standardized plans for specific camps, checking drawings and plans of other engineers, and supervising all phases of construction for the various projects in the district.

On March 30, 1944, Rogers officially resigned from his civil-service position with the corps for a position in private industry in Pensacola. Upon his departure he received a letter of appreciation from Lt. Col. J. T. Knight Jr., the district engineer, which praised his work as "the Chief Civilian in the Architectural and Structural section of the Engineering Division during the busiest period in the history of the office."[18] In fact, at the end of 1941, the Wilmington District office had had only 36 employees, with 210 assigned to field positions; by the middle of 1943, the office staff totaled more than 2,500 employees.[19] The letter also provides insight into Rogers' role in the office and the type of work undertaken by the office during the war period: "The care and judgment that you exercised in the site planning of a 14 million dollar camp (commencing with the initial Site Board Report), and in the coordination of the diverse and highly technical engineering phases of the work all speak for themselves as to your ability, not only as an architect and engineer, but also as an executive. The fact that the construction contractors were awarded the Army-Navy 'E' for excellence in construction at this camp has been a source of pride to the District."[20]

During the war period, the Wilmington District completed major construction projects in North Carolina at Fort Bragg, Camp Davis, Camp Butner, and Camp Mackall, as well as the construction of several air bases and airfields. The $14 million project referred to in Knight's letter most likely was the construction of Seymour Johnson Air Base near Goldsboro, North Carolina. This project involved the construction of the largest wooden hangar facilities in the country, which were completed under Rogers' direction. Over the next forty years, he continued to assist the Department of Defense and affiliated government agencies with construction solutions, including his report "World Wide Definitive Designs for Aircraft Hangars," examples of which were built from Langley, Virginia, to Seattle, Washington, and on overseas bases.

Rogers also assisted these agencies during the Korean War and was recognized individually by the chief of engineers for "Outstanding Service to the United States Army in Connection with Military Construction Activities from 1952 to 1959," for his firm's work on a variety of military designs, including highly technical facilities for the missile test center and the Gulf Test Range, part of the Air Proving Ground Center at Eglin Air Force Base near Valparaiso in the panhandle of Florida.[21] Today, Rogers' firm continues its close relationship with the Department of Defense and designs schools, housing, hospitals, and other facilities at bases in the United States and overseas.

The Second Phase

From February 1944 to the end of the war, Rogers worked for the Smith Shipyards in Pensacola, which was involved in designing and building tankers and landing craft for the military. The Marine Corps used the much-in-demand tracked landing craft as a means to secure islands in the Pacific theater. The private defense industry had grown tremendously in Florida during World War II. Many shipyards, including those in Tampa, Jacksonville, and Pensacola, provided supplies and equipment needed for the battles overseas, as well as for training at the many new military installations in the state.

Rogers returned to Winter Park in 1945 and resumed his practice in the Old Post Office building on Park Avenue. Rogers and his staff found the unair-conditioned space insufferable and therefore installed one of Winter Park's first air conditioners. Since there were no condensation lines, the staff devised a bucket system to collect the runoff and emptied it daily. Rogers stayed in the building for almost seven years, though he later complained of the poor construction, lack of insulation, and other tenants in the Old Post Office: "The building was put together with thumb tacks and glue, I guess, and you could hear right through the floor." Edith Royal's dance studio was on the first floor, and Rogers and his staff could hear the students "who were there in the afternoon: one, two, three—*kick*! One, two, three—*kick*! It nearly drove us crazy."[22]

In 1951 Rogers purchased land at the corner of Lincoln and Knowles Avenues from Dr. F. W. Nickel, a former client, and moved his offices there. Nickel sold Rogers the parcel for $3,000. Rogers designed his office building in about four days and within three months had moved out of the Old Post Office building.[23] In 1958 Rogers purchased the parcel adjacent to his property on the north for the purpose of expanding his offices. At the time, Rogers' staff was so crowded that they had been using the second floor of Taylor's Pharmacy on Park Avenue for additional operating space. The additional property, and the construction of additional office space, put the entire firm back under one roof.

After World War II, construction once again boomed, not only in Florida but around the nation. Rogers' firm, with its sizable staff, began to focus on commercial and government commissions. These jobs provided necessary cash flow for sustaining a larger office, while residential commissions made up a smaller portion of the project load. The in-house staff now held expertise in the disciplines of structural, mechanical, and electrical engineering and provided nearly complete construction services for its new clientele.

Small jails became a Rogers specialty. During the late 1930s Rogers had completed designs for county jails in Flagler, Pasco, and Volusia Counties. In 1946 he was commissioned to design the Calhoun County Jail in Blountstown, located in the panhandle of Florida. From the late 1940s through the late 1960s, Rogers' firm completed designs for more than fifty local, county, and state correctional facilities. Rogers wrote articles on the specific design requirements for such buildings and attended seminars dedicated to the discussion of jail design. His article "Modern Jail for Small County," published in the August 1957 edition of the *American City*, highlighted his design for the Taylor County jail in Perry, Florida. The jail consisted of an office, a wing that housed twenty-four prisoners, and another wing that provided living space for the sheriff and his family. The fact that a centrally located "cage" was used to house prisoners was, according to Rogers' article, preferable to the old system of cells located along jail walls. The cage system did away with the need to place bars on the windows—"bars are bad psychologically"—and also eliminated the "old-fashioned heavy, dark, Bastille-type of a prison and makes possible the use of an ordinary modern fireproof building."[24] Such mid-century alterations to prison design were the result of Rogers' study of the problem and his proposals to make prisons more humane and aid in the rehabilitation of prisoners. Rogers' Highlands County Jail, completed in 1956, in Sebring, Florida, won "Best Small Jail of the Year" in a national competition.

The Rogers firm also produced numerous designs for churches, courthouses, hospitals, apartment buildings, retail stores, and secondary education and university buildings. In 1945 Ray Greene, a Winter Park realtor and former mayor, commissioned Rogers to design two retail buildings at 114 South Park Avenue. The two-story masonry and stucco buildings provided retail space below, with small apartments, or flats, that could be rented above. The stores opened onto Park Avenue as well as onto a narrow walkway between the two buildings. The apartments were reached from a separate entrance on Park Avenue, or from an exterior staircase at the rear. (See color plate 1.)

While the buildings blend seamlessly with the rest of Park Avenue, they are notable for their narrowness—only nineteen feet wide—and for the use of clipped corners at both the front and back of the buildings. These clipped edges served multiple purposes. The first-floor space was designed to accommodate three separate stores, and the clipped edges of the buildings created corner entrances for the two end stores, while the middle commercial space was accessed by doors along the central walkway. On the upper floor, wrought-iron balconies extended from the clipped corners, providing the apartment dwellers with a small outdoor space. Rogers could have designed a box for the space—a building that covered the lot from side to side, facing full front onto Park Avenue. Instead, he met the needs of his client—a mixed-use facility—with the assumed desires of the building's tenants—separate entrances for each of the stores and an airy living space for the apartment dwellers above.

Greene, however, was not finished with his development of the lot. The next year, he commissioned Rogers to complete the commercial design with another mixed-use building at the back of the 130-foot lot, only a third of which had been developed in the earlier design. Like the front buildings, the rear building was two stories in height and took up the full 50-foot width of the lot, though it was only 30 feet deep. Retail space was provided on the lower floor, while the upper floor held apartments. The building possessed a more pronounced residential quality than the earlier buildings Rogers had designed for the lot, and many of the details of the balconies, frame supports, and shutters are similar to those the architect used on some of his Spanish-style houses. The arch in the staircase leading to the apartment balconies is similar to arches seen in the Barbour house, the Barbour Apartments, and the C. Griggs Plant house. Wooden casement windows rather than commercial windows were used in the building, and terra-cotta mission, or barrel, tiles covered the roof, which was outfitted with a false chimney—the quintessence of domestic living.

But the most notable element of the final mixed-use project was the creation of a courtyard between the two buildings, known as Greeneda Court. This charming open-air Spanish-style courtyard, complete with fountain, painted tiles, and curving stairs, is accessed by the narrow walkway leading from Park Avenue between the two street-facing buildings. The walkway is even further sheltered by overhanging trees and flowers. Beyond the rear wall of the stores, the space opens to the sky, although it is surrounded on all four sides by two-story walls. A pointed-arch opening pierces the back (east) wall with a walkway through the building to the cobbled street behind. The courtyard is fifty feet wide, the width of the commercial lot, and thirty-five feet deep; however, the space is enlarged by Rogers' use of clipped corners on the buildings surrounding the space. With this design Rogers created an enticing "secret" courtyard just off the bustling commercial strip of Park Avenue—one that continues to provide Winter Park customers with a place for a quiet respite—and he turned an otherwise ordinary commercial commission into one of Park Avenue's most alluring spaces.

The most important commission completed by the Rogers firm during the immediate postwar period was his design for the Florida Supreme Court Building in Tallahassee. In 1946 Rogers teamed with the Pensacola firm of Yonge and Hart to compete for four state-financed projects: a Supreme Court Building, a new 105-bed hospital at the historically African American Florida A&M College, a new State Road Department building, and the Millard Caldwell Office Building. Rogers' firm was responsible for the two former designs, while Yonge and Hart executed the latter two. Ralph Lovelock, who would later become a partner in Rogers' firm, was architect-in-charge of the design for the $2 million Florida A&M hospital, which was praised for its efficient layout and its design as an interracial hospital.[25] Rogers was in charge of the design for the Supreme Court Building, which was part of the 1947 Florida State Capitol Center Plan that proposed arranging state buildings on an east-west axis along Lafayette Street and on axis with the old Capitol Building, in which the Supreme Court had met since 1902.[26]

The Supreme Court Building was designed in the Classical style, a style traditionally associated with governmental buildings. Rogers may have drawn inspiration from similar building designs by John Russell Pope, especially his design for the National Gallery of Art in Washington, D.C. The temple front of the building is a six-columned pedimented Doric portico, above which rises a stepped dome. Three entryways, each with large double doors, lead into the central space, which is surrounded by eight columns of Maryland verde antique marble with white Ionic capitals and bases of Carrara marble. A marble replica of the Supreme Court seal is laid in the floor of the circular space. Doors beyond the domed rotunda space lead into the courtroom. Two-story of-

Plate 18. Florida Supreme Court Building, Tallahassee, 1946. Courtesy of RLF.

fice wings, with basement and subbasement levels, flank the center section. The use of the temple front and dome, with their historical and architectural associations with Roman precedents such as the Pantheon, emphasized the prestige and dignity of the court. Construction cost for the 50,000-square-foot building was $1.5 million.

On December 29, 1948, the Honorable Elwyn Thomas, chief justice of the Florida Supreme Court, presided over the dedication ceremonies for the new structure. The event was not without politics, as speeches were presented by Robert J. Pleus, president of the Florida State Bar Association; the governor-elect, Fuller Warren; and then-Governor Millard Caldwell, whose administration financed the project and who was later elected as a justice to the Florida Supreme Court. The actual address of dedication was given by Associate Justice of the U.S. Supreme Court Stanley Forman Reed. The building appeared on the cover of the 1951 edition of the *Florida Sheriff*, the annual publication of the Florida Sheriff's Association in Jacksonville.

In 1992 the Florida AIA awarded the Supreme Court Building its "Test of Time" award, given in recognition of the lasting value of good architectural design. More recently, the Supreme Court Building held the dubious distinction of serving as the backdrop for press conferences and political speeches during the recount of Florida votes in the 2000 presidential election.

In 1961 the St. Augustine Historical and Preservation Commission and the Board of County Commissioners approached Rogers for assistance in the redevelopment efforts under way in the historic section of that city. Since 1958 Rogers had been involved with efforts to restore St. George Street in St. Augustine to its Spanish Colonial appearance. His firm had acquired a reputation for authentic detailing and, as noted by the executive director of the Preservation Commission, was "nationally known for its work in precisely this kind of architecture and its competence in handling restoration work of this sort."[27] Rogers was asked to propose a plan for renovating Henry Flagler's Cordova Hotel into a new county courthouse. As early as the 1930s, there had been proposals for rebuilding parts of the Old City in St. Augustine along the lines of the "reconstruction" of Colonial Williamsburg, Virginia, and as the city approached the four-hundredth anniversary of its founding (1565), plans were once again rekindled. In 1962 the St. Johns County commissioners purchased the Cordova Hotel from the Florida East Coast Hotel Company. A four-year-long renovation ensued, and in 1968 the former hotel was dedicated as the county courthouse. Rogers' involvement with the process, however, ended in December 1961. It is unclear whether the 1960s renovation followed the recommendations set forth in his proposal. Ironically, the building was reconverted for use as a hotel in 1997 and is now the Casa Monica Hotel.

For nearly thirty years, Rogers operated his firm under the name of "James Gamble Rogers II," although he had taken on several additional architects. Before World War II, however, he had never formed legal partnerships with any of them. After World War II he took on architectural partners Ralph P. Lovelock and Laurance W. Hitt. During World War II Lovelock had worked with Rogers in the Wilmington corps office. Many of Hitt's detailed perspective renderings, executed in pencil, were used as presentation drawings for the firm's commercial, university, and governmental clients. During the 1950s Irwin W. Fritz, P.E., James A. Grinnan, P.E., and Herbert L. Clark, a specification writer, also joined the firm. In 1967 the name was changed to Rogers, Lovelock, and Fritz. Warren L. Chase was taken on as a partner in Rogers' firm in 1977. Until the early 1990s he served as head of the engineering division.

Both of Gamble's sons were also destined to join their father's architectural firm. James Gamble IV, "Jimmy," the oldest son, attended the University of Virginia for three years, studying architecture. When he left school, he came into his father's office and tried his hand at design. Although his father attested to Jimmy's design capabilities, he did not follow in the family business. Instead, he became nationally known as a folk singer as a member of the Serendipity Singers during the 1970s. Later, he left the group and moved back to Florida to concentrate on his career as a solo singer and storyteller. Jimmy, who chose the stage name of Gamble, produced numerous records and one-man shows, appeared on national television shows and at folk-music festivals, and had a regular segment on National Public Radio as a commentator. In interviews his father seemed to miss Jimmy's presence in the office, but always noted that the family was proud of him for doing what he loved to do. "I like his style," Gamble said. "He's not noisy. I don't like rock and roll."[28] In 1991 Jimmy died while attempting to save a drowning swimmer near his home off the coast of Flagler Beach. Each May the Gamble Rogers Folk Festival is held in St. Johns County, Florida, to celebrate his life and musical legacy.

In 1970 Gamble's younger son, John Hopewell, was made a partner in the firm. "Jack" graduated in 1962 from the University of Virginia's School of Architecture and soon joined his father's firm. Like his father, Jack seems to take the greatest pleasure in completing designs for residences, churches, and other civic buildings. Recently, he was instrumental in the effort to save the Barbour house from demolition. Successful in having the building moved to public property, he is serving as project manager in the house's restoration and renovation for use as a museum and home for the Winter Park Historical Society. The Rogers firm now has more than seventy employees, representing mechanical and electrical engineering disciplines, interior design, and architecture.

In the 1980s, as an octogenarian, Gamble Rogers received numerous awards, honorary degrees, and other honors for his role in shaping the course of Florida's twentieth-century architecture. Many business, educational, and social groups officially recognized Rogers' contributions to the field of architecture with organizational awards. Locally, he re-

Plate 19. Rogers in front of Olin Library, 1986. By permission of Department of College Archives and Special Collections, Olin Library, Rollins College, Winter Park, Florida.

ceived Rollins College's Hamilton Holt Award (1984), which recognized the architect as "a neighbor and friend, whose talents have given shape and character to our campus for nearly four decades," and he received the annual Outstanding Citizen award presented by the Winter Park Chamber of Commerce (1986). He had received status as an honorary alumnus at the University of Central Florida by the class of 1976, and in 1986 Rollins College likewise awarded him honorary alumnus status. The *Orlando Sentinel* referred to his "magical pencil" and its ability to transform pine scrub into architectural masterpieces, and the paper also touted his work as "Timeless Treasures."[29]

In addition, Rogers' work was exhibited at three retrospective shows, held at the Loch Haven Art Center in Orlando (1984), at the Cornell Fine Arts Center at Rollins College (1985), and at the Maitland Art Center (1985–1986). The show at Rollins College featured many of the 1920s and 1930s photographs taken by Harold Costain of Rogers' Winter Park and Orlando houses. In 1985 the Mid-Florida chapter of the AIA, which Rogers had helped to found in the 1930s, presented the architect with a "Certificate of Recognition for Contribution and Dedication to the Profession of Architecture." The chapter also awarded him a Medal of Honor in 1990.

Rogers, however, probably felt most satisfied by the acknowledgment he received from local residents and visitors alike, who felt a special kinship with many of his buildings, as though they held a personal stake in them. Clearly, Rogers' impact on the community went beyond the buildings he designed. Because of their contextual nature, the buildings became part of the larger community, rather than serving as individual, detached objects within the landscape. The result was that people recognized the intangible value these buildings gave to the built environment: scale, style, and grace. As his own work illustrates, Rogers was correct when he told an interviewer that "a good design is timeless."[30]

In 1980 Gamble Rogers retired from full-time work at his practice, leaving the daily operations to his son Jack. Gamble quipped that by being in retirement, he was down to forty hours of work per week. In reality, he usually worked a few hours in the morning, driving himself from his Temple Grove home in his old Volkswagen Beetle. He dabbled in some designs and made comments on others. He died in 1990, at his home. That year, he was made a Fellow in the AIA, posthumously.

3

Developing an Architectural Character in Winter Park

IN THE 1920s and 1930s James Gamble Rogers II was one of a handful of architects practicing in the town of Winter Park during the height of its development. Throughout his architectural career, Rogers exerted influence at local, regional, and state levels. Because of his keen eye for authentic detailing, Rogers' designs enriched Winter Park's aura of charm, culture, and art and supported the boosters' description of the town as "The City of Homes." His designs became the standard for new residences in the area. Regardless of the architectural style in which Rogers was working, he always adhered to certain design approaches.

Stylistically, Rogers believed that "architectural designs should be in harmony and should correlate with the general terrain and type of foliage that form the background for a town."[1] Aesthetically and practically, Rogers thought that the Spanish style of architecture was very well suited to Florida, where the climate and flora were similar to places along the Mediterranean, rather than to typical clapboard houses that were being constructed in the late 1920s. Rogers completed house designs in the Moderne and International styles, but preferred the historical revival styles that were nationally popular at the time. The architect considered himself a specialist in the Spanish and French Provincial styles, not because he studied extensively in those countries, but because he had studied the styles by observation.[2]

During the early part of the century, use of the Spanish style was being renewed in California and parts of the Southwest, as well as in parts of Florida, as American architecture looked back to its historical roots for inspiration. In general, the Colonial Revival movement celebrated the English roots most predominant in New England and in parts of the South. Other parts of the country did not share this colonial heritage. Instead, when they looked to their roots, they saw pueblos and Spanish Colonial architecture. Interpreting from these roots, movements such as Mission, Mediterranean Revival, and the Spanish Colonial Revival were born. The popularity of these styles increased through publications and events such as the 1915 Panama-California Exposition held in San Diego.

Although Florida retained little evidence of its Spanish Colonial past in built form, except in St. Augustine, there was a compelling economic reason to reinvent the state's Spanish history in newly constructed architecture. Beginning in 1885, Henry Flagler opened the state to tourism with his Florida East Coast Railway. With the outbreak of World War I in Europe in 1914, Florida easily filled the need for an exotic vacation destination and was heavily marketed to the wealthy social elite of New York, Boston, and Philadelphia. Florida quickly became known as the American Riviera, with a Mediterranean climate and Spanish-inspired architecture helping to fulfill that fantasy—ignoring the state's colonial ties to English and French settlements. Rather than conduct a grassroots search for identity, Flagler and developers like him romanticized the state's connections to this ancestry to the point of myth and reinforced the myth with their grand hotels that exhibited Moorish interiors and highly detailed exteriors. Since little authentic Spanish architecture survived in Florida, architects were free to use their imaginations as they built new resorts, new homes, and even new towns that often exaggerated, blended, and distorted true Spanish details.

Such stylistic freedom resulted in an imaginative interpretation, best referred to as Spanish Eclectic—often a blend of Spanish and Moorish architectural elements. Most commonly, these buildings were masonry structures finished in textured stucco. Although few window openings were evident on the facades, those that were present were deeply recessed, protecting the interiors from the heat of the sun, but allowing for cross ventilation from breezes. Windows were generally casement or double-hung sash units. Decorative windows, such as diamond-pane, stained, or bottle-end glass, were also used selectively. Doors were embellished with highly elaborate surrounds, and wrought-iron *rejas*, or grilles, were used at doors, windows, and balconies. The roofs were low-pitched hip or gables covered with terra-cotta barrel tiles or sometimes wood shakes.

Rogers also worked extensively in the French Provincial, or French country house, style. In general, this style features a variety of building materials, including stone, stucco, and wood, that are often combined in a form of half-timbering. Other hallmark elements of the style include steeply sloped roofs with bell-cast or flared eaves; casement windows, often with diamond panes and flanked on one side by wooden shutters; rounded turrets; and dormers. Rogers' own house, Four Winds; the

Camp house; and the Ingram house are examples of the French Provincial style.

Rogers also completed a large number of commissions in the Colonial Revival style, which has retained popularity up to present day. A broad category, Colonial Revival encompasses many house types, plans, and details. Most often, the house is symmetrically balanced in appearance, with a centrally located entrance, often featuring a pedimented porch supported by columns. Cornices and other classical elements were also used in the style. Most high style examples were clad with masonry, while vernacular examples were generally of wooden construction and cladding. As indicated, the Colonial Revival was a malleable style and was often adapted and modified.

In his house for L. V. Bledsoe, which was featured in *Architectural Forum*'s *The 1936 Book of Small Houses* and the April 1940 issue of *Better Homes and Gardens*, Rogers explained that the final design had been the result of "crossbreeding" the Cape Cod style of New England— a Colonial-inspired style "marked by simplicity, by compact room arrangement, and by low eaves that snuggle the house to the ground"— with other Colonial styles and architectural details.[3] The house was detailed with a simple cornice and a pedimented door surround with fluted pilasters and a full entablature with a decorated frieze. To this, Rogers added tall, narrow dormers and built the walls three feet higher than usual with the Cape Cod style, in order to raise the ceilings in the house. He also deviated from the typical rectangular plan of the Cape, creating an L-shaped layout, which made the house a bit more airy. The site of the Bledsoe house sloped down to Lake Virginia, and important rooms were placed on that side to take advantage of "both the view over the water and of the prevailing breezes from the southeast." The result was "a home of Colonial charm yet comfortable in a tropical climate."[4]

In addition to stylistic considerations, Rogers also tackled practical considerations that Florida residents faced. Aware of Florida's special climatic and ecological environments, Rogers imbued his designs with regional traditional qualities that made allowances for the intense Florida sun and heat and took strides to ensure constant air circulation. His early house plans almost without exception provide for a crawl space and, in many, a full-height basement—a rarity in Florida homes, given the high water table. This technique creates additional air circulation and moisture control. Raising the building off the ground, a method employed in Florida's vernacular Cracker-style buildings, also helps to prevent invasion by termites. The windows, transoms, and doorways

Plate 20. L. V. Bledsoe house as published in Better Homes and Gardens, *1940. Reprinted with permission from* Better Homes and Gardens. *Copyright Meredith Corporation 1940. All rights reserved.*

were arranged for cross ventilation of the spaces in order to capture any breeze that might be present. Windows in Spanish Eclectic–style houses had the further advantage of deeply recessed window openings, which provided bright but indirect lighting. In these ways, Rogers provided a comfortable environment for his clients in the days before central air-conditioning.

Aesthetically, Rogers' attention to materials, textures, and craftsmanship makes many of his designs works of art. In an effort to make his buildings appear timeworn, as though they had stood for years, Rogers often employed secondhand materials—a practice that today would earn him the label of "green" architect. As a practical matter, used bricks and tiles were a cost-effective measure during the Great Depression, but the practice also satisfied the architect's aesthetic desires. Lending an aged and romantic image to the building, these materials also provided rich and contrasting textures. A national architectural magazine commented that Rogers' work had "a mellowness of textures not often attained in a new house," a quality achieved, in part, by reusing materials.[5] Another softening, or aging, technique Rogers often employed in his Spanish Eclectic and French Provincial designs was the incorporation of an intentional sag in the ridgeline of the roof to create the illusion of decades, if not centuries, of settling. Rogers used this "antiquing" technique in his own cottage (Four Winds) on the Isle of Sicily, the Shippen house, the Barbour house, and the Noyes house.

Combining his artistic talents with his architectural skill, Rogers manipulated forms and spaces, adapting and mixing stylistic details to create a satisfying design, both aesthetically and practically. Rogers' interpretation of the Spanish style often leaned toward the Spanish farmhouse type, or *cortiljo*, catalogued in such publications as *Spanish Farm Houses and Minor Public Buildings* (1924) and *Provincial Houses in Spain* (1925). Rogers held these and other period books on provincial Spanish architecture, including Rexford Newcomb's *The Spanish House for America*, in his office library. Such books provided information on authentic details and the salient features of Spanish architecture.

Rogers' Spanish-influenced work exhibits such hallmarks of the style as second-story balconies that are often located in an interior courtyard, cantilevered from the main body of the house, and supported by large hand-hewn beams. The balconies often feature decorative wood railings, a detail directly descended from the Spanish Colonial style and often seen in homes in St. Augustine. Rogers also used decorative window types and openings, including bottle-end glass and grille covers for windows. As was typical with this style, the house was turned inward onto a courtyard, presenting few openings to the street. The mixtures of shadow and shade, bright but indirect light, and solidity with airiness were a result of Rogers' intention to make his designs responsive to the Florida sun, heat, and humidity.

The plans of Rogers' Spanish and French Provincial houses intentionally reflected the irregular scheme of an additive-type house. Rather than presenting an image of authenticity on the exterior while maintaining formalized plans on the interior, Rogers sought to imitate both the exterior appearance of the authentic precedent—farmhouses that were added on to as the family grew—and the additive feeling of the interior. This goal was achieved by such details as lowering the floor of adjacent rooms, separating rooms by small doorways, or tucking spaces into the corners of the overall design. Rogers, like Palm Beach society architect Addison Mizner, spent many hours designing every decorative feature of his houses, including lighting fixtures, decorative sculptures, and all wrought-iron decorations.

Rogers also considered the house's siting and surrounding landscape as very important features of his designs. Throughout his career he encouraged developers to plan large lots within Winter Park, since providing space between buildings protected the city from a cramped appearance. Vistas to and from the house were important to the design as well. The Barbour house is Rogers' best example of the integration of the architectural and landscape design. This integration was possible since Rogers was closely involved with Martin J. Daetwyler of Orlando, a landscaper Rogers had worked with in Fern Park. From Interlachen Avenue, the house could be seen across a wide lawn, while areas of subtropical plants were positioned throughout the estate. Rogers was unhappy with the landscaping installed by later owners, which included an earthen berm in front of the house that blocked the view from the street.

While it was Rogers' vision to create authentic architecture, it was the many craftsmen and builders that he worked with who brought the designs to life. In the early part of his career, Rogers was able to spend a great deal of time on job sites. This practice allowed him to resolve problems as they arose in construction by drafting design details on the site.[6] This close interaction between architect and builder led to a faithful execution of the designs. Harry C. Cone was Rogers' favorite local building contractor. Cone served as general contractor on many of the architect's Winter Park houses, including Rogers' own house and houses for the Shippens, the Casselberrys, the Barbours, the Bradleys, Mildred Mizener, the McAllasters, the Leonards, Mrs. Charles F. Schmidt, the Sanderses, and the Barbour Apartments. In Orlando, Cone was the contractor for the Ingram house, the Keene house, the Huttig house, and the Bingham house, among others. At one point both men had offices in the Old Post Office building on Park Avenue. Other contractors who worked on Rogers' local residences included Raymond A. Reynolds, William H. Waterman, and W. A. McCree. Based on the list of houses known to have been completed by each contractor, it appears that Cone was Rogers' choice for all houses that involved a significant amount of historically accurate detailing. The houses completed by the other contractors, while employing some detailing, were mostly modest Colonial Revival–style houses or houses that had very little applied ornament.

For the most part, Rogers' clients dictated the architectural style of his houses. Some of his clients, such as the Shippens and the Noyeses, came to him with a savvy understanding of architecture either through their own study or through personal experience and travel. These individuals often sought to participate in the romantic notion of the early

Spanish Florida and made specific requests for Spanish-style homes. Other clients, who were also architecturally knowledgeable and were seeking to demonstrate a progressive mind-set, desired a Modern-style house. The Jewett house and the Leonard house are examples of Rogers' attempts to satisfy these clients. Still other clients requested Georgian or Colonial Revival–style houses, possibly to assert their ties to an early American ancestry or to build in a familiar style in an unfamiliar environment. The Schmidt, Keene, and Bradley houses are examples of Rogers' Colonial Revival work. The remarkable point in this variety of styles is that Rogers was able to accommodate his clients' requests for each of these styles and to do it with seeming ease. Rogers was as adept at detailing a Spanish-style fountain as he was at detailing expanses of glass block. His talent seems to have been versatile and adaptable enough to accomplish these diverse designs as if expert in each.

Rogers' work set standards for excellence in design and detail through his interpretations of Spanish Eclectic, French Provincial, and American Colonial Revival styles. He helped to shape the architectural face of the young Winter Park with his designs, and today his buildings continue to be inherent to the town's national identity as a well-planned, aesthetically pleasing locale. The buildings are impressive alone, as objects, and the details are captivating in their exoticism. Yet, as a group of nearly one hundred residences spanning nearly seventy years of work, these buildings create more than romance. They form a community based on the value of good design and the recognition that each building plays a role—good or bad—in the image of that community.

Rogers' architectural talents led him to create a sense of place in Winter Park. The town was growing from its pioneering days of sand streets into a winter home for wealthy Northerners, a year-round vacation destination, and a full-time home for others. In providing buildings that were well designed, well detailed, and well sited, Rogers' work laid a framework for the town. Through his commitment to make his community a better place in which to live, James Gamble Rogers II gave to Winter Park a timeless treasure in his residential designs.

4

The Legacy

JAMES GAMBLE ROGERS II's architectural career spanned more than seventy years, during which he and his firm designed residential, military, health-care, educational, correctional, industrial, commercial, and religious buildings. As with Wright's work in Oak Park, Illinois, and Mizner's work in Palm Beach, Rogers' work in Winter Park created an architectural character for the town. It can be argued that the publication of many of his designs also exerted at least some influence on a national level by exposing Florida architecture to a national audience. Although Rogers worked in all parts of the state of Florida, his projects were not confined to Florida; in fact, he designed buildings in nearly every region of the country. Rogers viewed each of his buildings as a part of the larger community and, thus, part of a larger architectural and urban context. This awareness contributed to Rogers' desire to provide each client with a product that was pleasing but that also would contribute in general to the character of the community in which it was built. The fact that Rogers' buildings are some of the most admired and prized in the community is an indication that the architect was successful in fulfilling this ambition.

Rogers possessed the technical and artistic talent needed to become one of Central Florida's most respected architects. He had a proclivity toward fine artistic expression, as evidenced by his many detail drawings for construction documents, but he combined this talent with a refined sense of proportion, space, and human scale. Rogers' attention to detailing, the allusion to historical precedent, and the overall sense of spatial organization in his plans show a familiarity with the very principles being taught at the École des Beaux-Arts during the late nineteenth and early twentieth centuries. He also tackled such practical concerns for Florida residents as termite control, proper ventilation, and humidity control. The picturesque variety of building forms and materials and the transition between interior and exterior spaces are hallmarks of Rogers' work.

Notable in some of Rogers' designs is the use of indigenous materials such as pecky cypress, southern pine, and coquina rock, which demonstrates the importance of "place" in the architect's designs and his desire to use locally or regionally appropriate materials.[1] Additionally, the use of terra-cotta, brick, copper, wrought-iron, and leaded glass make his houses especially attractive and add interest to individual elements, as well as to the overall design. The details of the house never escaped Rogers. His attention was focused on every aspect of domesticity. Elements such as bookcases, mantels, and stair railings were custom designed, as were paneled doors, electrical fixtures, and wrought-iron work.

Stylistically, Rogers was inclined toward the historical styles of Europe, as adapted to the American lifestyle and Florida climate. He was not rigid in his use of styles, however, designing two houses in modern styles and using a stripped classicism with modern overtones in some of his designs for banks, hospitals, and art galleries. Yet it is for his work in the Spanish Eclectic style that Rogers is best remembered.

As most architects do, Rogers collected articles and books on specific architectural elements and stylistic details. He also had a file collection containing detailed photographs and drawings of mantels, masonry work, hardware, windows, and stairs. Most of these were gleaned from popular architectural magazines of the time, including *Architectural Forum* and *House Beautiful*. Rogers also held a large book collection that included volumes on modern construction practices as well as on historical architectural styles.

For Rogers, Florida was a perfect match to the warm and sunny climate of the Mediterranean, and his work reflects many of the quintessential elements of the Spanish house as described by Newcomb, such as the use of a *patio*, or interior courtyard.

The arrangement of a house on a site to maximize the interest of the view both from the house and of the house is comparable to Rexford Newcomb's description in *The Spanish House for America* of the Spanish tendency to utilize "enticing vistas to lend beauty to the house and make life therein more interesting."[2] Rogers' placement of windows, balconies, doors, and loggias was calculated to provide pleasing views from the interior of the house out to gardens, lakes, and even other portions of the house. For instance, the Plant house courtyard is surrounded on only three sides, rather than all four, and thus allows a view of the lake. Interior arrangements also were used to provide views from one space into another and involved such elements as corridors, stair halls, interior balconies, and interior courtyards.

Rogers was well aware of the established methods of good building techniques and cautioned against the negative outcome of poor construction. In his article "An Ideal for the Small Southern Town," Rogers acknowledged that the cost of building in Florida was less expensive than in the north, "but one of the greatest detriments to the establishment of good architectural standards is the habit of building too cheaply. Such things as central heating, weather-strips, proper insulation, and a good quality and sufficient number of coats of stucco are essentials to good building rather than luxuries. The services of a good architect are also a necessity. Too many buildings, particularly of the so-called Spanish type, have already been put up by builders or 'designed on the back of an envelope.'"[3] Rogers' implication was that often in architecture, once an image was determined, the designer walked away, leaving the details to someone else. Rogers believed that an architect should thoroughly delineate details of important elements in his working drawings, but field experience taught him that being on site was the best way to ensure the design was followed.

Rogers learned, though, that commercial projects were the way architects made more than a mere subsistence living. As his firm's staff size grew, he realized the importance of these more substantial projects: "Those are the things [commercial projects] that, if you're going to do any more in architecture than eke out a living, you have to get some commercial stuff because you simply can't survive on residences. When I was doing all those homes, I hadn't been out of college very long. I was doing all the detailing myself and probably earning about 25 cents an hour because the detailing is very important on these things. Otherwise, they look like stage scenery, you know that kind of thing—pasteboard architecture."[4]

Rogers' architecture went beyond the superficial image. In his Winter Park houses, we see how the architect responded to the Florida climate. He manipulated the exterior and interior elements in these designs to adapt to that climate, while also providing the client with the desired stylistic image. The character of these buildings does not rest solely with their architectural style. It is the collaborative effect of architecture and all its detail, the landscaping and its enhancement of the building, and the way in which the building addresses its context, be it urban or rural, that make these buildings special. Robert Bruce Barbour

Plate 21. Rogers, who was never without a boat to fill his idle hours, relaxes on the bridge of the Lotus, *a 42-foot Matthews cruiser, ca. 1970. Courtesy of RLF.*

saw Rogers' little French Provincial cottage on the Isle of Sicily and stopped to ask who had been the architect. Upon learning it was the owner, Barbour said, "I want you to design me a house." When Harold Costain saw the Barbour house as he drove through the streets of Winter Park, he said that he threw on the brakes and hurried back to look at the house and to photograph it. That house, now known as Casa Feliz, held such a special place in the hearts of Winter Park residents that when it was threatened with demolition, they picketed, raised money, and had the house moved and restored.

Rogers' work exudes an innate feeling of architectural "rightness," partly because of the extensive detail put into every aspect of the project, but also because the architect possessed a discerning nature about architecture and because he was seeking not only to add to the number of buildings in Winter Park, but also to improve the quality of the buildings in Winter Park. Retaining that character is an ongoing battle for preservationists and those who understand the uniqueness of Winter Park. Like many other places, Winter Park is struggling to maintain its character in the face of constant pressures to conform. Neighborhoods are changing as small cottages and modest homes are replaced by the construction of ever-larger houses that seem to occupy the entire lot and that are guarded by fences and walls.

Park Avenue, the central commercial district of Winter Park, began as a sand street containing wooden structures and horses. Today, it is an upscale shopping area anchored at one end by the artistic foundation of the Morse Art Gallery and at the other end by the intellectual institution of Rollins College. Rogers admired the architecture of Park Avenue and praised the buildings that evolved on the street over the years. Most buildings conform to a regularized setback, height, and material, giving a unified appearance to the street, while still allowing individual distinction among the buildings. As Rogers pointed out, "It's an example of what people with forethought and taste can do."[5]

5

Selected Houses

THE HOUSES IN this section have been selected in order to illustrate the different architectural styles in which Rogers was proficient, as well as the differing circumstances of each commission. The houses date from the late 1920s into the late 1930s, and all were designed for the Winter Park area.

Rogers House
1929

By the late 1920s Gamble Rogers had completed several residential designs through his father's firm. Some of these were in the Daytona Beach area, while others were in Winter Park and just north, in Fern Park. In 1929 Rogers took advantage of a unique business opportunity that resulted in the design of his own house. The house he designed for himself and his new bride, Evelyn, on Bear Island, now known as the Isle of Sicily, would be the catalyst for his architectural career in Winter Park.

This modest 1,800-square-foot house, which Rogers always referred to as his "cottage," was significant for several reasons. It was the first house to be built on the newly developed island, and the printed publicity the house received, as well as word-of-mouth interest, was a boost to Rogers' career. The house was also an example of the architect's skillful use of the French Provincial style of architecture as adapted to the Florida climate.

The story of how Rogers succeeded in securing the first lot on the Isle of Sicily and the subsequent construction of his cottage is best related by the architect himself, who memorialized the event in writing:

> After the collapse of the [Florida building] boom in the fall of 1925, building construction fell off to no more work than was necessary to finish work in progress. Land sales were zero and those

Plate 22. Rogers house, lakeside facade. Courtesy of RLF.

developers whose land and improvements were paid for could count themselves lucky.

The Isle of Sicily, so called by the developers, was originally a swampy island of about twelve acres in Lake Maitland. It was bought during the boom by Bob Hughes, whom I guess you would call a capitalist, Fred Wallich, an architect, and Judge Hackney, a retired winter visitor. These gentlemen filled the low land with sand pumped from the lake, paved a narrow road from Maitland Avenue, and built a wooden bridge spanning the 20 foot cut from the mainland. All this was in the period from late 1924 to about 1926. By the time the work was complete, the boom had collapsed and as the saying went then, you couldn't give land away.

When I first came to Winter Park to live, in 1928, I met Hughes and Wallich and although the island was only a sand spit with no living tree on it higher than my waist, I saw great possibilities in it. I told them that if they would give me an acre lot, I would lay out no more than twelve lots on the island and build a small house there for myself which would "stop the traffic." The only qualification was that I would be able to get electricity to the property. This was essential, since there were no utilities at all on the island.

They agreed, so I called Bob Orrell, a friend from Daytona Beach who owned a Sikorsky amphibian airplane, and asked him to fly me over the island so I could photograph it (with my limited funds, a twelve-acre survey was out of reach). I laid out a three hundred foot baseline on the white sand with black roofing felt and took sufficient photographs so I could plot the island within reasonable scale. The result was that the owners deeded me a centrally located lot, 165 feet wide, extending water to water, a depth of about 160 feet.

Although the house [Rogers' cottage] was published in seven architectural magazines and one book, it did not do as well for the developers as we had hoped—the second house was not sold until seven years later to Mr. and Mrs. Paul Burress, now the Tiedtke House.[1]

Rogers named his cottage "Four Winds," probably in reference to the breezes that the house enjoyed from all sides because of the openness of the island. According to Rogers' son Jack, the architect had chosen to build his home in the French Provincial style after he and Evelyn had seen a similar home on a trip to Macon, Georgia.[2] Of the more than one

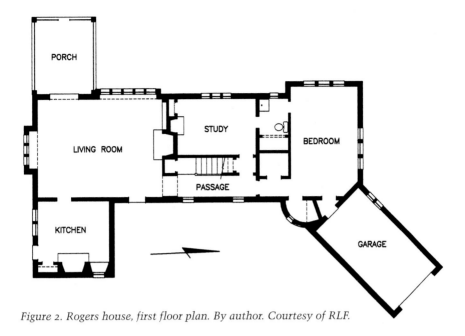

Figure 2. Rogers house, first floor plan. By author. Courtesy of RLF.

hundred homes Rogers designed in the Winter Park area, very few were built in the French Provincial style, although he stated on several occasions that the style was his personal favorite. Many of Rogers' clients came to him with a predetermined style for their houses, but when he was given a free hand, his admiration of the picturesque quality inherent in the French Provincial prevailed in his own home.

While the architect may have admired the style as seen elsewhere, the plan was clearly of his own design. In fact, the plan for the Victor N. Camp house, constructed about a year earlier in Ormond Beach, and Rogers' own floor plan are not unrelated. Both are essentially T-shaped plans featuring an entrance into the main living-room space, with the kitchen and dining alcove and master bedroom on the first floor, and guest bedrooms above. In his own house Rogers changed the location of the staircase from its tucked-away position in the Camp house to a more public area in the front hallway, or passage. Where Camp had two bedrooms on the first floor, Rogers used one space for a bedroom and the other as a study. Another difference in the plans was the addition of a turret at the north end of the long axis of the house to facilitate the angled transition into the canted garage space. Rogers also exposed roof framing in his own house rather than using the conventional flat ceilings of the Camp house. Perhaps in developing the efficient floor plan for the Camp house, the architect became so enamored of it that he used it as the basis for his own home with only a few minor alterations (fig. 2). (See plate 10.)

Four Winds was a small house by today's standards. The first floor consisted of one bedroom and one bathroom, a kitchen, living room, study, garage, and screened porch. From the street, the house appeared to be only one story in height, but Rogers had taken advantage of the very steep side-facing gable roof space by including a small second story, which consisted of a bedroom, bathroom, and dressing room. The house also had three fireplaces, two large ones in the rustic, Colonial-style kitchen and the living room and a smaller one in the study.

Photographs of the original kitchen were often included in publications about the house and show the space to be evocative of another era. The large cooking fireplace was flanked by a deeply recessed window on one side and a plank door on the other. A flat stone hearth fronted the fireplace opening, and a large wooden beam spanned the top of the opening, serving as the fireplace lintel and extending to serve as the sill of the flanking window. A built-in wooden bench was located on one side of the kitchen, and dark wooden beams were exposed along the ceiling. Other accoutrements included large cooking pots, cast-iron pans, candlesticks, and a lantern. The dark space could have been drawn from any number of eighteenth- or nineteenth-century French country farmhouses, and it is assumed that is what the architect intended. Adding to the authenticity of the space was the fact that the house had no heating system other than the fireplaces.

The two facades of the house, the street facade and the lake facade, were different in their use of fenestration. The building was sited to take advantage of the views of Lake Maitland from the living room, study, and master bedroom—all spaces on the west side of the house. Thus, the lakeside elevation included large groupings of windows, a shed dormer, and a screened porch. The street-side facade, however, featured only a few single casement windows. The "closed" nature of the facade was a technique that had its roots in many of the European revival styles popular at the time. Usually, the historical precedents were closed to busy streets on one side, but opened on the rear to gardens or courtyards. In Rogers' case, though the street was not very busy, the closed nature of the facade provided a good amount of privacy from any passersby (pl. 13). The rear facade, however, exhibited a much more open and less formal nature with its many windows and door openings (fig. 3).

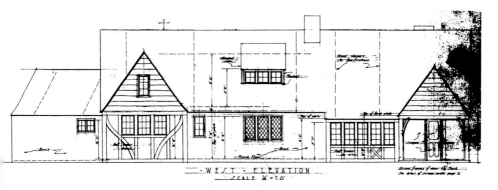

Figure 3. Rogers house, west elevation. Courtesy of RLF.

The house's structural system was wood frame, and the exterior was finished with a veneer of whitewashed stucco and whitewashed used bricks. On a section of the west (lake) facade, Rogers used half-timbering, typical of the French Provincial style. The house was covered by a very steeply sloped, sagging gable roof with cross gables at the ends. All exposed exterior wood elements—such as the rough-edged gable siding, roof shingles, doors, and window frames—were of local heart cypress. On the interior, the roof rafters and collar beams in the kitchen and living room were hand hewn, possibly of pine, and left exposed to the interior spaces. The interior trim work, such as the shelving and cabinets, was also of local cypress. The floors in the house were of random-width yellow pine, ranging from four to twenty inches wide.[3]

One of the most interesting features of the house was the rounded turret on the east facade. This was a favorite motif, employed by Rogers in many of his best projects in Winter Park, including the Barbour, Noyes, and Holt houses. As mentioned, at Four Winds the turret was used as a transitional form to join the skewed orientation of the garage with the more orthogonal orientation of the rest of the house. Functionally, the turret was used as a dressing room on the second floor and a closet on the first floor.

In 1937 Rogers made several changes to his house. Because the original house had no formal dining area, and because his family was growing, he renovated the existing kitchen into a dining room and added a new kitchen wing to the south end of the house. Within this addition a small stairway led to a second-story guest room and bathroom. A small furnace room was subsequently added to the north end of the house. At a later date the original cypress shingles were replaced with slate shingles.

The Rogerses lived in the house until 1949, when they moved to the Temple Grove estate between Palmer Avenue and Lake Osceola. Over the years, the cottage on the island underwent numerous additions and alterations, and in 1992 it was razed to make way for a larger house in its place. With this demolition Winter Park lost an important part of its history and an endearing work of architectural significance.

Although Rogers' plan for the Isle of Sicily did not pay off immediately for the developers, the house brought Rogers' design skills to the attention of Winter Park residents and others through its publication in several magazines, including *House Beautiful* and *Architectural Forum* and the *Forum's 1936 Book of Small Houses*. These publications praised the architect's use of the style following "a northern French farmhouse tradition," the handling of the materials, and the efficiency of the design. One criticism was the use of the turret space for a dressing room and closet, rather than a stair hall, which would have freed up more living space within the overall plan. Rogers heeded this recommendation in some of his subsequent plans that included a turret, including the Shippen house.

Four Winds also caught the attention of local residents, one of whom was Robert Bruce Barbour, who had noticed the distinctive cottage on the island and stopped to inquire who the architect of the house had been. This encounter led to the commission for the best known of Rogers' Winter Park houses, his 1932 Barbour house.

Shippen House

1931

In the Winter Park area, Rogers is best known for his Spanish Eclectic–style houses, with their stucco walls, clay tile roofs, and wrought-iron grills and balconies. Indeed, of the thirteen projects included in this book, seven are of this style. The first of these houses was designed in 1931 for Eugene Rodman Shippen and his wife, Elizabeth. Located at 1290 North Park Avenue, overlooking Lake Maitland, the Shippen house is an efficient courtyard-type design that displays the skillfulness of the thirty-year-old Rogers, creatively working in an historical style of architecture. (See color plate 2.)

Dr. Shippen was one of Winter Park's most distinguished citizens. He was born in 1865 in Worcester, Massachusetts, but spent a good part of his youth in Germany, where he said he acquired "a taste for German literature and music and beginning the study of Latin." He attended the

Roxbury Latin School in Boston and the Emerson Institute in Washington, D.C., and in 1887 graduated from Harvard University. He studied for three years at the Harvard Divinity School and for one year at Oxford (1893–1894) in preparation for the Unitarian ministry. Shippen held Unitarian pastorates in Kansas, Massachusetts, Pennsylvania, and Michigan. In 1900 he married Elizabeth Herrick Blount of Dumbarton Oaks in Washington, D.C.[4]

Elizabeth Blount Shippen came from a well-traveled and cultured family. Her father, Henry Fitch Blount, born in 1829, was a native of Ontario and became a successful manufacturer of plows and farm implements in Evansville, Indiana.[5] After the death of his first wife, with whom he had two children, Blount married Lucia Eames, with whom he had four more children. In 1886 Blount retired from his business at age fifty-seven, and took his family abroad for two years to live in France and Switzerland. In 1891 Blount became a vice president of the American Security and Trust Company, and Lucia was a charter member and secretary general of the Daughters of the American Revolution. Settling in Washington, D.C., Blount purchased the house at Dumbarton, along with six acres of surrounding land, when the Dent family was forced to sell off the property.

Elizabeth and her sister grew up in a stimulating environment. At The Oaks, the Blounts decorated the interior with items they had acquired while living in Europe. Particularly noteworthy was the family's set of Spanish *fraileros*, referred to by the family as the "Ferdinand and Isabella" chairs.[6] A family picture of Elizabeth and her sister shows the two reclining and reading in the ornately carved chairs. In addition to changing the interior decorations of the large house, the Blounts transformed the attic space into "The Little Theatre," where the Blount children gave performances for audiences of up to 200. As recounted in a history on Dumbarton Oaks, "the Blount girls had a lovely time planning decorations, raiding other portions of the house for stage sets and acting in plays that were written by friends of the family."[7] The household also enjoyed visits from venerable and popular personalities of the time, including Henry Blount's closest friend, Alexander Graham Bell; Andrew D. White, president of Cornell University; Clara Barton; Susan B. Anthony; Elizabeth Cady Stanton; Frederick Douglass; and Queen Liliuokalani of Hawaii.[8]

As a married couple, the Shippens traveled extensively, with one of their favorite destinations being Spain. Serving in various capacities to international religious conferences, Eugene Shippen traveled abroad more than fourteen times from 1927 to 1934. During one trip to the Middle East, he served as a "foreign correspondent" for the *Winter Park Topics* newspaper, detailing his travels and the people he encountered. Shippen once noted wryly that "all these trips abroad may account for my internationalism, which makes me suspect in certain quarters."[9]

Praising his wife's love of beauty and artistic creativity, Eugene Shippen said those qualities had "opened a new world to this New England Puritan, and have been a continual source of inspiration to me and to a large circle of friends."[10] In 1930 the Shippens moved to Winter Park and commissioned Rogers to design a residence for them. Considering their love of travel and Elizabeth Blount Shippen's cultured upbringing, it is little wonder that when it came to building their own home, they desired to express domesticity in such a richly historical and artistic style as the Spanish Eclectic. The couple's fondness for Spain also may have been the source of inspiration for their new home, which incorporated a wide variety of details from Spanish and Spanish Mission styles. The house was indeed a happy one, as it was the site of several family birthday parties and weddings.[11]

The Shippens were very active in the social and cultural life in Winter Park and may have met Rogers through these channels. Shippen was one of the original benefactors of the Mead Botanical Garden and was a founding member and the second president of the University Club. The couple had four children: Harold, an electrical engineer; Zoe, a portrait painter; Sylvia, a homemaker; and Rodman, a psychiatrist. In 1954 the Shippens donated the chapel furnishings for the new Unitarian Church in Orlando, which was designed by Rogers.[12] Dr. Shippen lived at his home on North Park Avenue until his death in 1959. He once credited his longevity to "a sound constitution, moderation, a happy domestic life, a cheerful religion, interest in progressive movements, and not least, twenty-five years of Florida sunshine."[13] After her husband's death Elizabeth Shippen moved from Winter Park to New Jersey to live with one of her daughters and died in 1966.

Located on a long and narrow site sloping northward toward Lake Maitland, the Shippen house is basically a U-shaped courtyard scheme that was designed as a series of overlapping stucco-clad forms featuring deeply recessed openings (fig. 4). The courtyard, which is on the south side of the house, is enclosed by an elliptically shaped masonry garden wall covered with stucco. A niche for a large urn or other statuary piece was located at the outermost point of the wall. In plan, the centerline of the ellipse in the wall is on axis with the center of the living room. A

Plate 23. Shippen house, view to northwest of interior courtyard. Photograph by author.

small fountain was another feature of the courtyard and was located along the same center axis.

The Shippens' house was constructed of hollow clay tiles on the first level and concrete blocks on the second level. The two-story mass was covered with a textured stucco finish. The numerous low-pitched gable roofs are covered with Mission, or barrel, clay tiles. The main gable roof, oriented east to west, has a four-inch sag incorporated into the ridgeline. The two-story gable roof over part of the west wing of the house is oriented north to south and has a three-inch sag incorporated into the ridgeline, while the one-story west-wing roof incorporates a two-inch sag. This technique, used to create an aged appearance, was used by Rogers in the Shippen house on a "sliding scale" that depended on the length of the overall ridge of the gable. The effect is subtle, but noticeable and effective.

Other elements on the exterior of the house include chimneys, a half-round turret, and deeply recessed window and door openings. The two

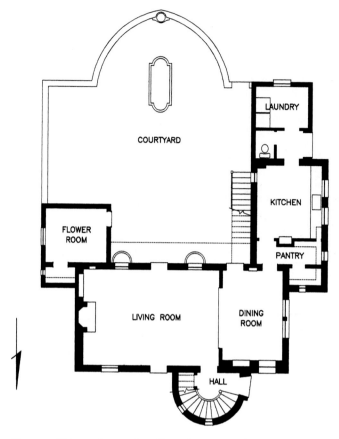

Figure 4. Shippen house, first floor plan. By author. Courtesy of RLF.

chimneys are simplified stucco-covered forms set flush with the plane of the exterior walls, with arched masonry caps.

The turret form was often used by Rogers as a transitional element in his designs and often contained the staircase. In the Shippen house the rounded turret, located on the north facade, encompasses the staircase but additionally serves as the main entry into the house. The turret roof, which is covered in Mission tile, is topped by a short six-sided cupola.

Adjacent to the turret on the north elevation, a slightly cantilevered portion of the second story is supported by six-by-eight-inch exposed timbers. The decorative use of these timbers, which do not serve a true structural function, simulates the Spanish Mission detail of carrying the ceiling beams to the exterior of the wall.

Plate 24. Shippen house, north facade. Photograph by author.

Because of the twelve-inch-thick hollow clay tile walls on the first floor of the house, Rogers was able to deeply recess the door and window openings, creating shadows in sharp contrast to the white stucco exterior walls. Most of the windows are single or double casements, with the exception of the turret windows, which are bottle-end glass with leaded frames.

The deeply recessed window and door openings are decorated with typical Spanish elements. The entry door to the house is made of pecky cypress boards with elaborate wrought-iron studs and a small sliding wood panel inset from which to view visitors. Many of the windows have decorative wrought-iron box grilles over them, while other windows originally had wooden shutters flanking them.

The Shippen house balconies also merit attention. The small cantilevered wooden balcony located on the west side of the house, and facing the street, is covered by a barrel-tile shed roof. The columns supporting the roof are five inches in diameter and are turned, or "twisted." This element gives the west facade a sense of spatial relief and visual dimension and creates sharply contrasting shadows against the white stucco wall surfaces. A larger cantilevered balcony is located on the south side of the house, overlooking the courtyard. It features hand-hewn heavy timber framing and can be accessed by an exterior staircase. Originally, the timber of both balconies was stained a dark brown, again presenting a contrast with the white exterior stucco.

The first floor plan of the Shippen house is designed as a series of overlapping rectangles with the addition of a semicircular stair hall. As mentioned, one enters the house through the rounded turret, which is located on the north side of the living room. Within this space the wrought-iron railing along the winding staircase cascades toward the front door and entry foyer. (See color plate 3.) An arched opening to the south leads into the living room, the largest room on the first floor, which is characterized by a flat ceiling featuring two large exposed hewn beams and a fireplace on the east end with a simple molded surround and no mantel. Doors and windows provide access both to the courtyard on the south and to the yard and lake on the north. The floors in this space, as in most of the house, are random-width pine. To the west and on axis with the center of the living room is the dining room, which is elevated by two steps, giving the space a more intimate atmosphere. Together, these three rooms (entry foyer, living room, and dining room) create an integrated sequence of compact yet balanced spaces.

The kitchen and laundry room are contained within the one-story west wing of the house. The east wing is comprised of a small flower room accessible only from the courtyard. The second floor plan of the house consists of three bedrooms. The master bedroom, which shares a bath with another bedroom, features a shallow fireplace centered on the east wall and double-leaf, or French, doors on the south wall, which lead to the balcony overlooking the courtyard. The third bedroom, located in the west wing, is accessible only from the courtyard staircase and was probably used as a maid's quarters.

The Shippen house is typical of the Spanish Eclectic style in that it exhibits an austere simplicity on the exterior, while also presenting a contrast of textures, materials, and colors. Thick stucco-clad walls, a rounded turret, carefully arranged and deeply recessed openings, wooden overhanging balconies, and rounded roof tiles are all hallmarks of the style. In this design, Rogers shows an ability to manipulate the forms and individual elements of the style into an understated but well-balanced design. Built for a couple with grown children, the house was a modest 2,300 square feet. The unassuming nature of the house, however, is part of its charm. The house provided a happy environment for the Shippens, their children, and grandchildren for nearly thirty years.

Barbour House

1932

Measured by almost any standard, Rogers' greatest achievement in residential design is the Barbour house of 1932. Designed for Mr. and Mrs. Robert Bruce Barbour, this Spanish Eclectic–style house was originally located at 656 North Interlachen Avenue. Although it is a relatively early work for Rogers, considering his long and prolific career, it is nonetheless his preeminent house design. Perhaps this accomplishment was made possible at least in part by the unusual circumstances surrounding the project.

Barbour, a native of Lansing, Michigan, came to Winter Park in 1915 from Chelmsford, Massachusetts, where he was the owner of the Eclipse Chemical Manufacturing Company which made indelible inks and aniline dyes. For the first eighteen years of his residence in Winter Park, he lived at New England and Chase Avenues.[14]

In 1932, after seeing Rogers' own French Provincial–style residence on the Isle of Sicily, Barbour commissioned him to design a Spanish

Plate 25. Barbour house, view to east. Photograph by Harold Haliday Costain. Courtesy of RLF.

farmhouse on Lake Osceola. As Rogers relayed the story of the commission: "Mr. Barbour came to my house on the island and asked, 'Who is your architect?' I told him and he said, 'Well, I want you to design me a house. I don't want anything like this at all. I want a Spanish farmhouse. You go ahead and design it any way you want. I'll limit you to cost and number of rooms, but I'll not interfere with you at all while you are designing the house. You do it any way you want and if I don't like it, I'll sell it.' It was an architect's dream come true."[15]

The plans for the Barbour house were drawn in 1932 at John A. Rogers' branch office in Winter Park. In February 1933 a groundbreaking ceremony was held, at which one hundred friends and neighbors gathered on the Barbours' lakefront lot, including Rogers, who displayed a clay model of the proposed building.[16] The fact that the house was completed during the depth of the Great Depression did not quell Barbour's interest in the project. He felt that the conditions actually favored him and that he would be able to get better prices on labor and materials because of it. In fact, because of the economic hardship of the time and the eagerness of the city to stimulate business, Barbour was granted a three-year respite from ad valorem taxes (personal property taxes) if he started construction right away. Total construction cost for the fifteen-room, 5,400-square-foot house was $25,000.

From its completion in 1933, the Barbour house played a significant role in the architectural and cultural contexts of Winter Park. Barbour and his wife, Nettie, were greatly involved in the social life of Winter Park and often graciously volunteered their home to clubs and organizations for meetings and social gatherings. Among the various activities centered around the house and its grounds were Garden Club tours, Symphony Orchestra concerts, Florida Poetry Society meetings, and a dinner for the Pulitzer- and Nobel-prize-winning American author Sinclair Lewis. In 1938 the house was the site of the Spanish Institute of Florida (Instituto de las Españas) annual fiesta honoring Cervantes. The two-day celebration featured an "Andalusian evening" (Noche Andaluza) with music furnished by the Spanish Symphonette and the Spanish Serenaders.[17] The event must have been successful, since the institute held its annual meeting at the house the following year, as well. Later owners would name the estate "Casa Feliz," the name by which the house is locally known.

While Rogers insisted that the Barbour house was a replica of an Andalusian *cortijo*, or Spanish farmhouse, the architectural style of the house is best described as Spanish Eclectic, since it incorporates not

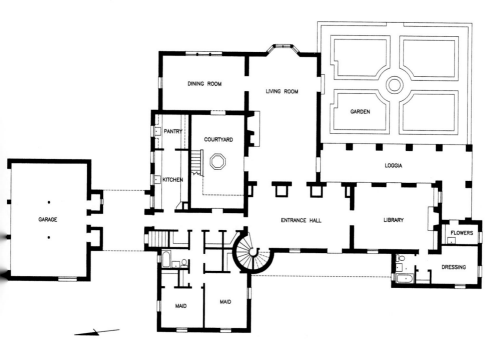

Figure 5. Barbour house, first floor plan. By author. Courtesy of RLF.

only authentic Spanish details but also elements inspired by other Mediterranean styles. In its plan the house indeed resembles a *cortijo*, which historically was a house type that was periodically enlarged as a family grew and additional space was needed. This characteristic is exemplified in the Barbour house through the rich variety and combination of forms used in the building mass. The organization of the house is a series of rectangular spaces centered around an interior courtyard (or *patio*), which closely follows the archetypal precedent. The open court, surrounded on all four sides by interior living spaces, is a common element of residential designs throughout the Mediterranean.

In *The Spanish House for America*, Rexford Newcomb expresses the physical and spiritual centrality of the courtyard to the Spanish house design: "a 'Spanish' house without its *patio* is no longer a Spanish house."[18] Newcomb contrasts the interior courtyard scheme of the Spanish house, wherein a "shaded retreat deep within the house, yet open to the air and light" was provided, to the residential planning of northern European countries, in which a dooryard or garden stood between the house and the street. In the Barbour house, Rogers combined the two modes by using the authentic planning device of an interior courtyard enclosed on all sides by the house, but also providing an extensive lawn between the house and the street.

The west facade of the building, which faced Interlachen Avenue, consists of four major elements: a pointed arch; a rounded turret; a heavy timber balcony; and a bell tower (pl. 26). The pointed arch separates the garage from the main body of the house. It is continuous through the width of the building and was constructed from cast segments of concrete. To simulate age and use, Rogers actually chipped away pieces of concrete from the edges of the archway (pl. 27).

The 125-foot length of the house is emphasized by a series of low-pitched gable roofs that are oriented north to south. As he had done in his previous two houses in Winter Park, Rogers incorporated a six-inch sag in the ridgeline of the main gable roof of the Barbour house.

The rounded turret is another element that Rogers used many times in his early designs. The Spanish houses he completed for George C. Holt, George L. Noyes, and Eugene R. Shippen all incorporated this element. He also used the turret in non-Spanish designs, such as his own home on the Isle of Sicily. In most of these examples, the turret was used as a stair tower, as it is in the Barbour house. The rounded turret form in combination with the more rectangular forms of the building provide a picturesque quality to the design.

The heavy timber balcony, centered over the front entry of the house, is characterized by hand-hewn timbers (beams, columns, and rafters) of pine stock (pl. 28). The entire balcony is cantilevered from the upper level of the masonry wall. The balusters of the balcony railing, which are turned and painted alternating colors, and the carved-block column capitals were the only timber elements to receive any type of decorative treatment. The posts and beam supports exhibit only the hewing marks of the carpenter's adze (pl. 29).

In traditional Spanish houses, balconies were most often provided over a *patio* and served as open-air corridors. A gallery, similar to a balcony but usually supported by a solid wall or piers, was a common element used on the front facade of houses, especially in Catalonia, and, as Newcomb points out, presented an additional variation of "shade-producing inventions."[19] Beginning with St. Augustine houses in the seventeenth century, American versions of Spanish house designs adapted the use of the front balcony to provide an additional space that was open to the outdoors but shaded from the intense sun.

An element unique to the Barbour house was the use of broken brick arches to terminate the west end of a long loggia at the southwestern

Plate 26. Barbour house, view to northeast. Photograph by Harold Haliday Costain. Courtesy of RLF.

Plate 27. Barbour house, detail of pointed arch. Photograph by Harold Haliday Costain. Courtesy of RLF.

Plate 28. Barbour house, front balcony and turret. Photograph by Harold Haliday Costain. Courtesy of RLF.

corner of the house (pl. 30). The loggia, which overlooked a formal flower garden and the lake beyond, could be accessed by double-sash doors from the entrance hall, living room, or library (pl. 31). More than any other detail, the broken arches in this design illustrate Rogers' desire to simulate the appearance of a timeworn building—in this case, even to the point of ruin.

In maintaining the character of the Spanish style, Rogers used a variety of distinctive window types and covers. The two windows in the stair tower are made of bottle-end glass set into leaded frames and were manufactured by Frank Armstrong of Casselberry.[20] The remainder of the windows are wooden multipaned casements arranged in pairs. Wooden or iron grilles, or *rejas*, were typically used in Spanish designs to bar the exterior of first-floor windows. At the Barbour house, Rogers used a concrete grille placed flush with the wall plane at the opening near the front door. Since the window opening is deeply recessed, the space between the grille and the window becomes a cool, shaded space through which breezes may pass. A wooden grille of turned spindles, a more common Spanish type of window covering, was used over a win-

Plate 30. Barbour house, detail of broken arches. Photograph by Harold Haliday Costain. Courtesy of RLF.

Plate 31. Barbour house, view looking northwest at arched loggia. Open doors lead into living room. Photograph by Harold Haliday Costain. Courtesy of RLF.

Color plate 1. View looking north through Greeneda Court, Park Avenue, Winter Park. Photograph by Rich Franco.

Color plate 2. Shippen house, view to northeast. Photograph by Rich Franco.

Color plate 3. Shippen house, view from living room to stair hall. Photograph by Rich Franco.

Color plate 4. Holt house, east facade. Photograph by Rich Franco.

Color plate 5. Holt house, detail of east facade, showing recessed entry, second-story balcony, and turret. Photograph by Rich Franco.

Color plate 6. Holt house, living room, view looking east. Photograph by Rich Franco.

Color plate 7. Jewett house, view to northeast. Photograph by Rich Franco.

Color plate 8. Burress house, view to southwest. Photograph by Rich Franco.

Color plate 9. Burress house, view to north. Photograph by Rich Franco.

Color plate 10. Burress house, living room, view looking south. Photograph by Rich Franco.

Color plate 11. Plant house, view to southeast. Photograph by Rich Franco.

Color plate 12. Plant house, view from living room toward reception room. Photograph by Rich Franco.

Color plate 13. Mizener house, view to north. Photograph by Rich Franco.

Color plate 14. Mizener house, stair hall. Photograph by Rich Franco.

Plate 32. Barbour house, entrance hall. Photograph by Harold Haliday Costain. Courtesy of RLF.

dow in the garage. Wooden shutters with Z-shaped supporting bars, an element less common in authentic Spanish designs, were another window component Rogers used at the Barbour house.

The round arched doorway and paneled door of the house lead into the large entrance hall. Rogers used this formal element, which was seen often in Mizner's Palm Beach mansions, in only a few of his larger residential designs. Given that the Barbour house was intended for social and cultural events, an entry space was needed that would accommodate many people. The stairs, enclosed within the turret, are located at the northwest corner of the entrance hall, while the living room, accessed through two arched openings, lies directly to the east. A bay opening, leading to a terrace, is located at the east end of the living room and allowed a view of the lawn and Lake Osceola. Doors on the south wall of the living room opened to the formal gardens and the brick-arched loggia. The living room's north wall features an opening into the interior courtyard, a fireplace flanked by a small wall niche and an arched opening into the formal dining room (pl. 33). Hand-hewn wooden rafters

Plate 33. Barbour house, north wall of living room. Photograph by Harold Haliday Costain. Courtesy of RLF.

and collar beams were left exposed in the ceilings of both the living room and the dining room. An opening south of the entry hall leads to the library, which features built-in wall niches for bookshelves and a fireplace on the south wall. These four spaces—entry hall, living room, dining room, and library—made up the public domain of the house.

A passage leading directly north from the entrance hall connects with the wing of the house containing the maids' rooms, the kitchen, and the pantry. The three-car garage, with vehicular entrances on the north side, was separated from the main body of the house by the aforementioned pointed archway. A basement with a small furnace room, which had a full-height ceiling, was also included in the design beneath the maids' room and the entrance hall. The basement was later converted into a wine cellar.

The second, more private floor of the house is composed of four bedrooms arranged around a large central hall. Double-leaf doors open from the hall to the wooden balcony located above the main entrance to the house. The two innermost bedrooms both access an internal L-shaped balcony, which overlooks and is accessible to the interior courtyard be-

Plate 34. Barbour house, interior courtyard. Photograph by Harold Haliday Costain. Courtesy of RLF.

low. Local newspaper descriptions cited the interior courtyard as "one of the pleasing features of the house," with a private stairway leading from the patio to the owner's suite of rooms on the second floor.[21] The courtyard was entirely surrounded by other living spaces of the house: the living room on the south, the dining room on the east, the kitchen on the north, and the passage wall on the east.

Rogers' desire to give the house an aged appearance dictated the materials selected in construction. The Barbour house is constructed of solid, twelve-inch-thick masonry load-bearing walls clad with second-hand, whitewashed brick obtained from the old Orlando Armory, which was razed about 1930. Although most Spanish houses employ stucco over masonry, Barbour insisted that the brick be left exposed.

The use of barrel, or half-rounded, tiles on the gable roofs of the house also adds to the textural quality of the exterior. Rogers procured the clay tiles from Penney Farms, near Jacksonville. In 1925 James C. Penney, founder of the J. C. Penney department store, and his partner, Ralph W. Gwinn, purchased 120,000 acres in Clay County near Green Cove Springs. On part of the land known as Long Branch, and later called Penney Farms, Penney set about to construct a community of cottage apartments for retired religious, social, and educational administrators and workers. Housing was free of charge. By 1930, though, Penney had been caught in the bust that followed Florida's boom, and although he presented the Penney Farms community corporation with a quit-claim deed to the property and buildings, many of the residents were forced to leave.[22]

The buildings Penney constructed at the retirement community were designed in a French Norman style. It is not clear why the company would have purchased barrel tiles for use with this style, which commonly uses flat terra-cotta roof tiles. Still, according to Rogers, he bought the tiles for the Barbour house from Penney Farms when the corporation was trying to stay afloat. The handmade tiles had been purchased from a roofing salesman who had toured Cuba in the early 1920s, trading tin for tiles. The salesman was told that the tiles had originally come to Cuba from Barcelona, where the peasants made them over their thighs, giving them just the right taper.[23]

Interior furnishings for the Barbour house were also selected with great care. The Barbours secured the skills of Mabel Noyes, who was hired as "consulting decorator" to travel to Spain in order to retrieve furnishings for the house. Noyes stated that "from the moment that Mr. and Mrs. Barbour asked me to help them select the furnishings for their lovely house I tried never to lose sight of the fact that it was to be the home of twentieth-century Americans, not seventeenth-century Spaniards. With this idea in mind we worked for an atmosphere of comfort, color, harmony, and a certain air of subtle distinction which is so well achieved by the judicious use of a few fine examples of antique art."[24] The antiques they purchased may have included chairs, tables, tapestries, benches, and cabinets seen in period photographs of the interior taken by Harold Costain. Rogers added custom designed electrical fixtures, including metal lanterns and sconces. All rooms were finished with plain plaster walls and random-width oak flooring.

Two sculptural elements at the Barbour house were also custom made. Rogers designed a highly decorative arched surround for the front door and wanted to incorporate carved or cast figures into the scheme. Nothing found locally satisfied the architect, so he contacted George Etienne Ganiere, Rollins College professor of plastic arts (1929–1935). On a trip to Rome, Ganiere had made a plaster cast, or "squeeze," of a lion's head sculpture at the Vatican. Rogers commissioned Ganiere to

Plate 35. Barbour house, living room, looking southwest. Furnishings selected by Noyes. Photograph by Harold Haliday Costain. Courtesy of RLF.

produce two concrete casts of the squeeze and placed these at either side of the front entry of the Barbour house.[25]

The Barbour house replaced the Ergood house, a three-story frame dwelling with a dome-topped tower that was constructed on the site in 1895. The lot that surrounded the former Queen Anne–style house was heavily wooded when Barbour purchased it. As part of his overall design, Rogers worked with Martin J. Daetwyler to transform the lot into a more open, scenic landscape. The site had been cleared of about 200 trees, which were replaced with tall palms, palmettos, bamboo, and subtropical foliage plants. The grounds also included a lily pond and a large pool that flowed over into several stepped goldfish basins and eventually into the lake.[26] Newspaper accounts observed that the wide expanse of open front lawn "gives the house a breadth of perspective unusual even in Florida" and provided an unencumbered view of the house from the street.[27] Later owners installed a landscape berm with trees and shrubs in order to obtain some privacy from that very view of the house. The architect expressed his disappointment in this change since the house was designed to be seen from the street.

In 2000 the Barbour house was threatened with demolition when new owners found the house's rooms too small for their needs and wanted to demolish the existing structure to build a larger house "in the Addison Mizner style."[28] In order to preserve the house, the Friends of Casa Feliz was organized and raised enough money to have the house moved across Interlachen Avenue to public property at the edge of the municipal golf course. The house is currently undergoing restoration and when completed will be available for special events. The Winter Park Historical Association also will have offices in the house.

The move has actually provided an opportunity to restore many of the original features of the house that had been lost over time because of alterations and additions. Most significantly, the broken arches along the rear loggia will be restored to their original "ruinous" condition. Former owners had filled in the arches to create an additional living room. The house is also once again visible to the public and will once again serve as a social and cultural hub for Winter Park residents.

Barbour Apartments
1938

Closely related to the Barbour house are the apartments at the southeast corner of Knowles and Swoope Avenues, designed by Rogers for Robert

Bruce Barbour in 1938. Barbour was interested in "giving Winter Park the most attractive apartments in Florida," with the "charm of old Spanish architecture."[29] After his residential project of 1932 was so highly acclaimed, Barbour commissioned Rogers to design a series of seven apartments that would re-create a "street in old Spain."[30] By 1938 Rogers was well versed in the architectural language of the Spanish Eclectic style, having designed at least six such houses in the Winter Park area. Barbour once again proved a very amenable client and told Rogers, "I had so much fun building this house, I want to build an apartment. I want to build a Spanish apartment and, again, want you to build it. You can build it any way you want, but get me six or seven or eight apartments in the building."[31] In the Barbour Apartments, Rogers responded with another artistic composition of stucco forms in this style. The apartments were well received, and in the winter of 1938 seasonal visitors were already leasing them. The prime location of the apartments added to their appeal. The municipal golf course, Park Avenue, the principal winter hotels, and Rollins College were mere blocks away.

The overall arrangement of the building is a two-story L-shaped form with a courtyard. The complex is actually two separate linear buildings joined by a celebrated portal entry, providing access into the courtyard. One of the most interesting aspects of the Barbour Apartments is the dichotomy expressed in the articulation of the courtyard (interior) and street-side facades. The exterior, or street, facades are given a distinct Spanish appearance through the use of stucco walls, clay-tile roofs, deeply recessed windows, towers, spires, arches, gateways, wooden shutters, and wrought-iron window grilles. On the courtyard side of the building, however, the Spanish theme is replaced with a more contemporary image of large expanses of glass. Rogers' original courtyard elevations show a far more cohesive design that continued the use of typical Spanish elements. The modern expression on the courtyard facade is the result of Barbour's desire to provide ample light and air for the residents, as well as to provide an economical means of construction in an area less seen by passersby. A local newspaper article describing the new apartments called this a "realistic response to the demands for maximum sunshine and air in the modern manner" and encouraged the new tenants to "sit outside and enjoy the sunny garden with its orange trees and azaleas."[32]

The most distinctive feature of the building complex is the large gracefully arched stairway on the exterior of the west facade, facing Knowles Avenue (pl. 36). It is a beautiful expression of form, with its sinuously

Plate 36. Barbour Apartments, view to southeast. Photograph by author.

curved and stepped outer wall. The backdrop to this staircase is a heavily textured coquina rock gable end wall with a single chimney at the peak of the gable and a recessed arched opening to one of the upper apartments at the top of the stairs. To the right of this wall is the entry portal to the courtyard, with tile roof and stucco spire.

The building is constructed of hollow clay tile that is covered in textured stucco, except for the aforementioned coquina rock wall on part of the west facade. The various hip, gable, and shed roofs, as well as the courtyard portal, are all covered in half-round Mission or barrel clay tiles.

Each of the seven apartments contains a separate covered entry, a large living room, one or two bedrooms, one or two bathrooms, a kitchen, dining alcove, and various storage areas. Several of the apartments also have an open porch conducive to Florida living. No two apartments were of the same plan, and three of the units were two stories, providing extra bedrooms above.

Although changes have been made to the interiors of the apartments, such as kitchen remodelings, the beauty of the exterior has remained virtually unchanged. Rogers did design other apartment complexes later in his career, including Greeneda Court, a more urban, mixed-use complex on Park Avenue.

Noyes House

1934

The house designed for George and Mabel Noyes at the corner of Interlachen and Swoope Avenues is the most idiosyncratic of Rogers' Spanish Eclectic projects in Winter Park. It is essentially a 2,500-square-foot, one-bedroom house with an office and art studio and a side court-yard. No formal dining room was included in the plan. Designed in 1934, the Noyes house is a far more urban response than Rogers' other work in Winter Park and maintains hallmarks of Spanish precedents combined with Rogers' own artistic touches.

The eccentric nature of the house reflects the personalities and ac-tivities of the couple for whom the house was designed. At the time Rogers designed the house, George Loftus Noyes was a well-known American impressionist painter, whose upbringing and educational training had exposed him to a wide variety of cultural influences. Noyes was born in Ontario in 1864. His parents had moved from Vermont fol-lowing employment in the oil industry. When Noyes' father died, his mother moved with her three sons to East Cambridge, Massachusetts, and operated a boarding house.

Despite their meager earnings, Noyes' mother encouraged her sons to pursue the arts. George learned to play the cello and was painting by the age of fifteen. In 1885 he was listed in Cambridge directories as a decorator and was employed by the local glass company to paint flowers and objects on their products. Around 1890 Noyes left Boston to study in various ateliers in Paris. He spent a summer painting the French countryside, where he discovered his lifelong passion of plein air paint-

Plate 37. Noyes house, view to northwest. Photograph by Harold Haliday Costain. Courtesy of RLF.

ing. In 1892 Noyes returned to Boston, where he established himself as an independent artist, frequently exhibiting his work at the Boston Art Club and the Boston Society of Water Color Painters. His paintings of exotic subjects completed while traveling in Mexico with Frederic Edwin Church received critical acclaim.[33]

In 1900 Noyes rented a studio in Annisquam, Massachusetts, on Cape Ann. There, he met his friend's sister-in-law, Mabel Winifred Hall, who was an accomplished pianist. The two shared mutual interests in art, music, and decorating. In 1903 they were married at Annisquam. From 1903 to 1906, Noyes taught drawing and painting at Stanford University and spent summers in Annisquam. After reportedly losing "practically all that he had in the world" in the 1906 San Francisco earthquake, Noyes returned to Boston, where he continued to define his own style of landscape impressionism. In 1915 he was awarded a Silver Medal in painting at the Panama-Pacific Exposition held in San Francisco.[34]

Around 1932 the Noyeses moved to Winter Park from Boston and lived at 642 North Interlachen Avenue before commissioning Rogers to build their new home. George Noyes' work had been the subject of an exhibition, "Paintings of Spain," at Rollins College. Mabel Noyes presented an informal lecture at the opening of the exhibit, which also featured Spanish and Italian antiques from her personal collection. According to family history, Noyes moved to Winter Park to teach at Rollins College and hoped to be appointed as director of the college's art department.[35] Rollins archives, however, do not list Noyes among the faculty, nor do they contain information to support the latter assumption, but clearly the artist had anticipated staying in Winter Park for a while, since he commissioned a house design from Rogers.

During their years in Winter Park, the Noyeses were often listed among the guests at various art exhibit openings, and they participated in the lectures and exhibits held at the Woman's Club and at Rollins College. Mabel Noyes operated her decorating business, Aux Tours D'Argent, from a shop at 354 East Park Avenue. An advertisement for the shop lists her as "consulting decorator," and she received much publicity for her role in furnishing the interior of the Barbour house with authentic Spanish antiques.[36] It is likely that through their involvement with the Barbour house, the Noyeses were inspired to commission their own home from Rogers.

Rogers described the Noyes house as a Spanish city house, which

Plate 38. Noyes house, courtyard and turret. Photograph by author.

traditionally presented something of a bare wall to the street. While the main entrance into the house is located on its east facade, facing Interlachen Avenue, the primary focus of the house is directed toward the distinctive courtyard space located on the south side of the dwelling. The stucco-clad south facade forms a backdrop to the courtyard and is articulated by a gabled portico and a rounded turret, which is the most prominent feature on the exterior. A U-shaped stuccoed wall encloses the courtyard, and an arched opening along the south side of the wall provides access from Swoope Avenue. Many spaces in the house—such as the foyer, living room, staircase, second-story loggia, and shop—have either physical or visual access to this courtyard.

The exterior materials used at the Noyes house are typical of the Spanish style. The entire house and the walls enclosing the courtyard are clad with stucco, and the low-pitched, multileveled gable roofs and rounded turret roof are covered with terra-cotta barrel tiles. The front facade, or *fachada*, as described by Newcomb, reflects the Spanish urban tradition of having few openings. Rogers enlivened this austere, nearly eighty-foot-long wall plane with decorative wrought-iron window grilles, wooden shutters, gable roofs supported by heavy timbers, and a small second-story balcony.

Plate 39. Noyes house, detail of window grille. Photograph by Harold Haliday Costain. Courtesy of RLF.

The wood-frame structural system of the Noyes house is comprised of two-by-eight-inch exterior wall studs covered in textured stucco. The thickness of the wall studs is probably dictated by the fact that Rogers wanted the windows and doors to be deeply recessed. It is unclear why he specified frame construction instead of masonry on this project, but cost may have been a factor. The roof framing in the living room is made of hand-hewn four-by-six-inch rafters and collar beams exposed to the interior. A full-height basement, an uncommon space in Florida houses, was located beneath the kitchen area and was used to accommodate a heating furnace.

The largest and most elaborate space on the first floor is the double-height living room. This dynamic space is the first example in which Rogers carefully integrated a staircase turret, a second-story balcony, and a large angled ceiling space together as the main living area. The space is brightly lit through three casement windows and transoms located on the south wall. The dark wood of the ceiling and balcony are thus contrasted against the white of the stucco walls. A bottle-end glass window in the turret, located at the southwest corner of the room,

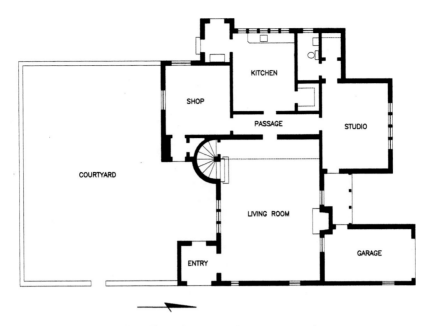

Figure 6. Noyes house, first floor plan. By author. Courtesy of RLF.

lights the wooden stairs. The architect would use this sequence of spaces later, in his designs for the Burress and Holt houses, but he would modify the details.

Other notable spaces on the first floor include a painting studio and a shop. Before moving her decorating business to Park Avenue, Mabel Noyes probably operated from her home shop, which had its own entrance from the south courtyard. Clients could park on Swoope Avenue and enter the shop without ever entering the private home, although the Noyeses' house may have been used as a showplace for some of Mabel's antiques. Rogers' construction drawings indicate that several decorative elements of the house were to be provided by the owners, including the living-room mantelpiece, the exterior balcony off the upstairs dressing room, the double-leaf plank and wrought-iron front door, and an exterior plaster ornament placed in the gable end of the front facade.

George Noyes' painting studio, accessed through a passageway located west of the living room, was a nearly square room that projected from the north side of the house. Four casement windows with transoms above pierced the north wall of the space and provided bright but indirect lighting for the artist. The studio was a self-contained area of

Plate 40. Noyes house, detail of front door provided by owners. Photograph by author.

the house, with its own bath and a closet. An exterior door connected the studio space, via a heavy timber loggia, to the garage, located at the northeast corner of the house.

The rooms on the second floor—a master bedroom and dressing room—are accessed from the second-story interior balcony, which overlooks the living room below. The floor plan was balanced by centering the arched entrance to the bedroom with the center of the balcony, thereby visually maintaining a central axis throughout the design. A door on the south wall of the bedroom leads to the gallery, an element valued in Spanish designs as an exterior shaded living space. The Noyes gallery, which overlooks the shop roof and exterior courtyard, features plastered columns and a canvas-covered floor. The space is covered by an extension of the house's main gable roof. Wall niches and small notched openings in the gallery wall lend interest to the porch.

The Noyes house was created for two artists who greatly admired the beauty and picturesque qualities of the Spanish style. The house reflects the clients' request for separate working areas within the house plan. The decorating shop accommodated clients with a separate entrance, which was enhanced by the presence of a formal courtyard; the painting studio, also with its own entrance, was oriented to provide northern light for the artist. In addition to supplying his clients' programmatic requirements, Rogers incorporated into the house hallmarks of the Spanish style in the selection of materials, decorative elements, variation in floor heights and roof heights, and overall arrangement of forms and spaces. The Noyeses stayed only a few years in Winter Park, moving to Vermont in 1936. The house was purchased by Tracy Lay, who in 1939 commissioned an addition from Rogers.

McAllaster House

1934

The McAllaster house, located at 160 Alexander Place, is one of Rogers' most logically and efficiently organized Spanish Eclectic designs. Built for Archibald and Lena McAllaster in 1934, the house possesses a subtle and pleasurable entry sequence not found in any other Spanish Eclectic design created by Rogers.

Plate 41. McAllaster house, view to east. Photograph by Harold Haliday Costain. Courtesy of RLF.

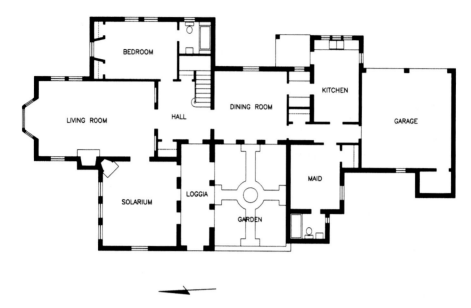

Figure 7. McAllaster house, first floor plan. By author. Courtesy of RLF.

The clients' building lot was located on the east side of Alexander Place, which is a narrow street running north from New England Avenue to a circular turnaround. A small park is located at the end of the street, at the southern edge of Lake Osceola. The McAllasters' lot fronted onto the street and sloped northward to a line adjacent to the public park overlooking the lake.

The house is basically a U-shaped courtyard scheme; however, in the McAllaster plan the courtyard is placed at the front of the house rather than at the back, as in the Barbour house, or the side, as in the Noyes house. In placing the courtyard forward, but maintaining its enclosed nature through the use of tall stucco garden walls, Rogers made the outdoor space part of the graceful entry sequence to the house. This sequence is begun by entering through a gated, arched opening punched into the wall plane. The opening leads to a heavy timber loggia, or arcade, which is covered by a shed roof. The courtyard, with its formally arranged flowerbeds, fountain, and sculptural pieces, lies south of the loggia. The design of this outdoor room creates a pleasing place for the visitor to pause and adjust from the intense sun to the cool shade of the house (pl. 43).

Rogers included numerous architectural elements within this courtyard *sala*, all of which were intended to physically, as well as visually,

Plate 42. McAllaster house, loggia entryway. Photograph by Harold Haliday Costain. Courtesy of RLF.

cool the visitor in the interval between the gated opening and the actual entrance to the house. Given its orientation, the loggia would have been set in shade year round. The brick of the floor and the whitewashed brick of the house wall and loggia arches are intended to reflect this coolness and provide variations of dark and light within the space. The dark wooden rafters and decking supporting the shed roof over the loggia are exposed and create a rustic, informal character. The sight and sound of the water splashing in the fountain and the coolness afforded

Plate 43. McAllaster house, courtyard. Photograph by Harold Haliday Costain. Courtesy of RLF.

by the grass and tropical foliage planted in the courtyard add to the sensual experience of the entry.

A second-story timber balcony with hewn columns and decorative capitals is cantilevered over the courtyard and serves to cast additional shadows onto the west facade of the house, to draw the visitor's eye upward, and to enhance the enclosed nature of the courtyard. This balcony is similar in detail to the front balcony at the Barbour house, though it was completed on a smaller scale (pl. 44). The scale and proportion of each of the entry elements and the symmetry that connects them indicate that even at this early point in his career, Rogers had already developed a keen sensibility to space and the ways in which architecture can affect the emotional and physical response to a space. The combination of the loggia, courtyard, and balcony creates an intriguing street appearance for the house, since only parts of each can be glimpsed from that vantage point.

The exterior materials and elements used at the McAllaster house are all drawn from the traditional lexicon of Spanish Eclectic design. The house is of frame construction clad with a veneer of whitewashed brick. The multilevel, low-pitched gable roofs are covered with clay barrel tiles. Like the Barbour and Noyes houses, the McAllaster house was clad with tiles that Rogers had acquired from the Penney Farms retirement community. Rogers used an elaborate wrought-iron grille over the window closest to the street, which complements the wrought-iron gate in the adjacent arched entry. Concrete grilles, flush with the wall plane, were used on the second-story window openings.

At just over 3,000 square feet, the house is of a moderate size, yet it contains four bedrooms and five exterior balconies. The first floor plan wraps in a U shape around the courtyard and includes the major public spaces. A first-floor bedroom and a two-car garage, respectively located at the northeast and southeast corners of the house, are spaces that protrude from the main rectilinear form. The stairs are a standard switchback type—that is, the stairs climb to a landing, then turn and proceed to the second floor in the opposite direction. Placed in the entrance hall directly in front of the main doorway, the stairs provide an efficient and centrally located organizing element within the plan. The stairs are a much more prominent element of the house scheme than the turret-enclosed stairs that Rogers often tucked into the corner of a space, as at the Barbour house.

The three major spaces of the first floor plan radiate from the entry hall: a first-floor master bedroom, the living room, and the formal dining room. These spaces were efficiently laid out to accommodate daily usage as well as formal entertaining. To the north, the double-leaf doors of the living room visually extend the house toward the park and lake beyond. The formal dining room is located south of the entry hall. The western wall of this space holds three double-leaf, multipaned doors that open onto the courtyard, again blurring the line between interior and exterior spaces. A passage leads south beyond the dining room to the kitchen, maid's room, and garage. The garage was later renovated into a less formal family room.

The solarium, located on the north side of the entry loggia and accessed via the living room, was the most elaborately detailed space on the first floor of the McAllaster house. This space, also used as a library, incorporates hand-hewn ceiling rafters and collar beams and a masonry fireplace with a rounded mantel in the northeast corner, an unusual placement more commonly seen in Mission-style designs. As its name implies, the space is brightly lit with three pairs of casement windows on the north side and three double-leaf doors, each aligned with an arch on the loggia, on the south side. Within the overall design of the house, the solarium plays several roles. As a form, it projects westward from the main portion of the house toward the street and, thus, provides spatial relief along the front facade. It also creates the loggia through a shed extension of its gable roof and acts as one of the four walls that enclose the courtyard. As built, the solarium was probably one of the most pleasant spaces in the house, since it had views of the lake, the courtyard, and the street.

On the second floor, Rogers was able to efficiently provide three bedrooms and two full baths. The largest of the bedrooms overlooks the lake to the north. Another of the bedrooms accesses the balcony that overlooks the front courtyard. Though modest, the rooms were arranged to provide the residents with pleasant views and cooling breezes.

The floors of the house are of both oak and pine—oak was used in the more public spaces, while pine was used in such areas as the kitchen and bedrooms. A full-height basement, constructed of concrete block walls, is located beneath the entry hall.

Closely related to the McAllaster design is the Ingram house, which is located at the corner of Marks Street and Laurel Avenue in Orlando (pl. 45). When the McAllaster house was featured in a national home magazine, Mrs. L. C. Ingram called Rogers and asked him to replicate the house for her. Rogers was not eager to produce two identical houses

Plate 44. McAllaster house, view from second-story balcony. Photograph by author.

in the same community. He did agree to design a house with the same floor plan, but delineated the exterior in a different architectural style.

In the Ingram house, which was completed in 1935, Rogers returned to the French Provincial style and added a few Venetian touches, replacing, element for element, the Spanish style of the McAllaster house. The simple arch of the McAllaster entryway was replaced with a trefoil arch with double chevron surrounds (pl. 46). Instead of barrel tile, wooden shakes covered the roofs. As with his other French Provincial designs, Rogers incorporated sags into the roof ridges at the Ingram house. In place of the heavy timber balcony, Rogers designed a balcony with diagonal braces and wooden lattice. Modifications to the floor plan were minor. Instead of three doors opening from the solarium onto the loggia, there was only one, and the columns of the arcade were detailed with a band of projecting brick that served as a type of capital. The courtyard, which in the Ingram house became "the cloister," featured an open-air garden with a centrally located fountain and brick pathways. The space

Plate 45. Ingram house, view to southwest. Photograph by Harold Haliday Costain. Courtesy of RLF.

Plate 46. Ingram house, detail of doorway. Photograph by Harold Haliday Costain. Courtesy of RLF.

Plate 47. Ingram house, detail of arched openings into cloister. Photograph by Harold Haliday Costain. Courtesy of RLF.

was surrounded on two sides, rather than just one, by an arcade. The street side of the arcade featured three pointed arches set on a brick half wall and separated by cast columns with composite capitals.

Some elements did not change between the designs: both houses were of frame construction clad with a veneer of whitewashed brick, and Harry C. Cone was the building contractor on each. Rogers probably enjoyed the challenge of creating a new image for his design. In later years the architect cited the Ingram house as among his favorites. Photographs of both houses taken by Harold Costain were published in several magazines, including the 1938 issue of *Florida Architecture and Allied Arts.*

Harris House

ca. 1936

Unbuilt

The unbuilt Percival Harris house represents another return to Rogers' early French Provincial designs, such as the Traylor house in Fern Park, the Fern Park Post Office, and his own home on the Isle of Sicily, Four Winds, which was completed seven years prior. As mentioned, the French Provincial was Rogers' favorite architectural style, with its hallmark steep roofs, turret forms, and variety of exterior building materials, including brick, stucco, and the combination of both in half-timbering. As shown on the construction drawings, the Harris house was to be located on the south side of Via Lugano, the street that leads to the Isle of Sicily. The site plan, one of very few provided by Rogers on his early drawings, shows the residence on a large lot situated between Via Lugano and Lake Maitland.

Percival Harris was a real estate salesman for the Floyd-Lindorff Realty Company in Orlando. He had lived at 337 Interlachen Avenue until 1936, when he moved to 600 Via Lugano. Though this location corresponds to the lot as shown on Rogers' site plan, it is known that the Harris house was never built here.

The house was proposed to be built of frame construction clad with a veneer of whitewashed brick, stucco, and half- timbering. The most prominent exterior feature of the house is the stucco-clad rounded turret form capped by a bell-shaped tile roof. The tile prescribed for the house was a flat clay tile and is believed to be the first such use for Rogers. He would later use the same tile on the Burress house on the Isle

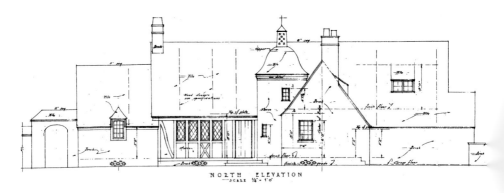

NORTH ELEVATION
—SCALE ¼" = 1'0'

Figure 8. Harris house, north elevation. Courtesy of RLF.

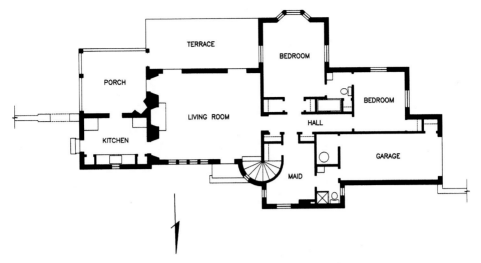

Figure 9. Harris house, first floor plan. By author. Courtesy of RLF.

of Sicily. A dovecote in the shape of an obelisk and a weather vane capped the turret of the Harris house and thereby increased its height. A dovecote was a domestic detail often seen in French country homes.

Other elements that bear similarities with the design for Four Winds include the intentional sag in the ridgeline of the roof, the sections of half-timbered wall surfaces, and the inclusion of a heavy timber screened porch. On the Harris house, Rogers designed a six-inch sag in the main east-west gable roof and proposed four-inch and three-inch sags in the house's minor roofs. Half-timber work was depicted on the street facade of the house, while a heavy timber screened porch featuring a fireplace and hewn cypress members with diagonal braces was to be located at the rear of the house. Other materials included wavy-edged horizontal cypress siding in the gable end walls. Stylistic components of the design included casement windows, French doors, and a variety of roof dormers.

The first floor plan of the Harris house was designed as a linear sequence of spaces from the kitchen on the east end of the house to the garage on the west. Lacking a formal entry space, the house is entered directly into the living room, which has steeply pitched, exposed roof framing and a second-story balcony overlooking the space. The balcony is accessed by a semicircular stair enclosed within the turret form, which was located directly adjacent to the entry. A fireplace with a heavy timber lintel and a simple bracketed mantel was located at the east end of the living room, opposite the balcony. This spatial relation-

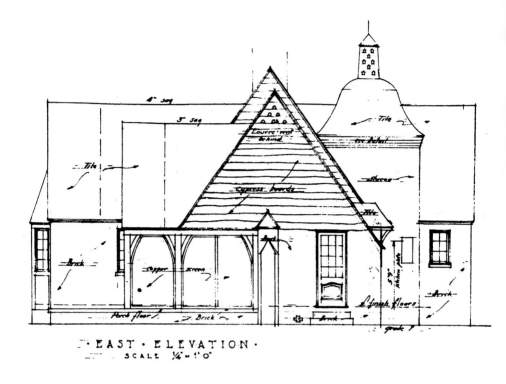

Figure 10. Harris house, east elevation. Courtesy of RLF.

ship between the living room, second-story balcony, and curving stair was similar to that in the Spanish Eclectic–style Noyes house designed two years earlier.

Other spaces provided on the first floor included a modest kitchen, two bedrooms that shared a bath, a maid's room, and a terrace accessed from the living room. A single-car garage was attached at the west end of the house with a catslide, or curved, gable roof. As with other houses of this period, no formal dining room was provided. Most likely, a dining area was informally incorporated into the living room, which was connected to the kitchen. The second floor plan consisted of the balcony space overlooking the living room, another bedroom, and a storage room.

The plans of the unbuilt Harris house show a highly developed but traditional design in the French Provincial style. Rogers' compact 2,100-square-foot, two-story house efficiently provided ample living space for its residents, but it also provided a generous public space in the living room, which was extended to the outdoors through the screened porch and terrace (fig. 10). The exterior materials and forms were also common to Rogers' previous work. In the modest but artistic Harris house, the architect combined these tested elements into a cohesive design that was never to be realized.

Holt House

1937

The Spanish Eclectic–style house at 1430 Elizabeth Drive is actually the result of two separate designs by Rogers. Originally designed in 1937 as a two-bedroom home for George and Rebecca Holt, the house was more than doubled in size by a substantial addition designed for the Holts by Rogers in 1941. The cohesiveness and sense of balance Rogers attained with this residence make it one of his most picturesque Spanish designs—a remarkable feat considering the difficulty of adding on to an existing structure. (See color plate 4.)

George Chandler Holt, born in 1907 in New York City, was the son of Hamilton Holt, who served as president of Rollins College from 1925 to 1949. Under the senior Holt's leadership, Rollins embarked on a construction campaign that established the Spanish building theme at the school. He was also responsible for revising the curriculum and raising the college to its position as one of the country's leading liberal arts institutions. In 1931, after transferring from the Taft School in Watertown, Connecticut, George Holt received a B.A. from Rollins College. While at Rollins, Holt was a four-year member of the tennis and crew teams, served as chairman of the Student Curriculum Committee, served on the student council, and sang solo bass in the Glee Club for two years. He was also a member of the Rollins players, a theatrical group. From 1931 to 1934, Holt was a Rhodes Scholar at Oxford University, where he studied politics and economics, and he later studied at the University of Geneva, Switzerland.

Upon his return to the United States, Holt taught at a preparatory school near Tucson, Arizona. In 1936 he accepted the position of dean of admissions at Rollins College. In this role Holt was responsible for interviewing prospective students and for the direct supervision of all details concerning the admission of students. During this time Holt was also chairman of the college's Committee on Educational Survey, which wrote the report on which the present curriculum of the college was founded.[37]

In 1936 Holt also met Rebecca Ann Coleman, daughter of Mr. and Mrs. Benjamin Ray Coleman. Rebecca had completed preparatory work at the St. Katherine School in Davenport, Iowa, and then attended Rockford College in Illinois for two years, before receiving a degree from Rollins in sociology. In Chicago, where her father was a business leader and city commissioner, Rebecca performed social welfare work at the Episcopal Church's mission of health. In Winter Park, where her parents had a home on Alberta Drive, she worked with the Junior Welfare Association in Orlando and the Junior Benefit League of Winter Park. Because Holt and Coleman were members of the "younger social set," the announcement of their engagement was a significant event in Winter Park. Upon their engagement, the couple announced plans to "build a Spanish or Mediterranean house in Winter Park."[38] Gamble Rogers was a likely choice as architect given his stature in the community and his personal relationship with the Holt family.

Located on a wide lot sloping toward Lake Osceola, the Holt house is composed of a central two-story mass flanked by a linear arrangement of low one-story masses nestled into the landscape. The two most prominent elements on the front facade of the house are the second-story balcony cantilevered above the entrance and the rounded turret form. The three-bay, heavy timber balcony, supported by cantilevered and shaped six-by-six-inch beams, provides a deep shadow and sense of spatial relief against the solidity of the masonry on the east-facing facade. The roof of the balcony, an extension of the main gable roof, is covered with barrel clay tiles. The rounded turret is the key to Rogers' successful addition to the original house. It is a form that the architect used many times to enclose a staircase, as in the Barbour and Noyes houses. In the Holt house, however, the turret was used strictly as an aesthetic device to form a transition from old to new. The turret was located at the end of the old garage space, which was then renovated into a small study and bar. A short, stucco-clad, octagonal cupola, which was covered with barrel tile, capped the turret. (See color plate 5.)

Other notable stylistic elements on the exterior of the house include a deeply recessed entryway flanked by tall, elaborately paneled wooden shutters; casement windows and double-leaf doors; both wrought-iron and turned wooden window grilles; and four painted brick chimneys with decoratively shaped caps.

The Holt house was constructed of concrete block exterior walls that were not stuccoed, but simply painted. This is the only Spanish Eclectic–style house Rogers designed that was finished in this manner, and

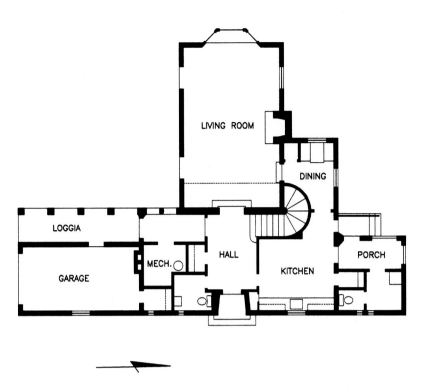

LIVING ROOM

DINING

LOGGIA

HALL

PORCH

MECH.

KITCHEN

GARAGE

Figure 11. Holt house, first floor plan, 1937. By author. Courtesy of RLF.

the choice may have been economically driven. Two other residential designs by Rogers, the Leonard house and the Jewett house, also had painted block walls; however, these designs were executed in modern styles that lent themselves to such a stark expression of materials.

The 1937 design for the Holt house was a compact, T-shaped arrangement terminating at its south end in a one-car garage. Rogers used the integrated sequence of entry hall, double-height living room, staircase, and second-story balcony that he had previously used in the Noyes house design as the central organizing concept for the plan of the Holt house. Of particular interest is the roof-framing system in the double-height living room, in which four-by-six-inch rafters supporting the roof are exposed to the space below. Attached to every third pair of rafters is a metal tie rod incorporating a decorative metal turnbuckle detail. These tensile members are used in place of the more typical collar beams, to resist the outward thrust of the rafters. (See color plate 6.)

In 1941 Holt commissioned Rogers to enlarge the house to accommodate his growing family. At this time the garage was converted into a study, and a long wing with three bedrooms and two bathrooms was

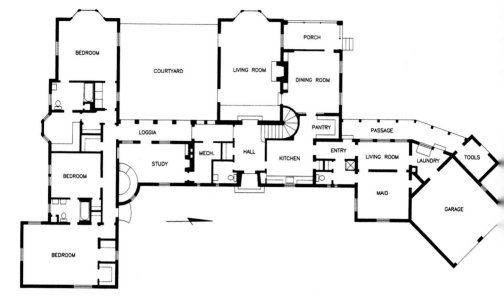

Figure 12. Holt house, first floor plan, 1941. By author. Courtesy of RLF.

added to the south end of the house. The bedroom wing in conjunction with the existing living room and loggia formed a U-shaped courtyard overlooking Lake Osceola. At the same time, a formal dining room, maid's quarters, a two-car garage, a trunk room, a laundry room, and an open loggia were added to the north end of the house. Despite the numerous spaces dictated by Holt for the 1941 addition, Rogers was able to achieve a tremendous sense of balance and cohesiveness among the many forms. The size of the house was increased from 1,800 square feet to nearly 4,000 square feet of living space.

Holt, who divorced in 1943 and remarried the following year, remained at the Elizabeth Drive house until the late 1940s. He and his family then moved to the Holt family farm, known as "Dogpatch," in Woodstock, Connecticut. From 1948 to 1950, Holt served on the staff of Connecticut Governor Chester Bowles and then became a personal assistant to industrial designer Norman Bel Geddes. In 1952 George Holt became executive director of the North East Branch of the United World Federalist, an organization that he helped to found, and executive director of the Grenville Clark Institute for World Law, an organization that espoused Holt's long-held belief in greater world unity and peace through a world government. Holt died in 1969 after a long illness and was survived by his wife, Dorina, three sons, and a daughter. A memorial service was held in his honor at Knowles Chapel on the Rollins College campus.

At the Holt house, as in Rogers' other Spanish Eclectic designs, the style dictated the architect's choice of materials and forms. Rogers used traditional barrel tile on the roof, which adds to the textural appearance of the house and creates a rich color contrast to the light-colored concrete block walls. Deeply recessed openings and a front balcony also added shadow and dimension to the walls.

Rogers' mature sense of spatial relationships in residential design is apparent in the Holt house. The sequence of spaces from the entry foyer through the west end of the living room (a part of the original 1937 design) is a compelling spatial composition. Through the use of axial relationships, overlapping spaces, and detailing, Rogers was able to integrate the entry hall, staircase, balcony, and double-height living room into what would become a hallmark of his early interior spaces.

Jewett House

1937

In 1937 Dr. Eugene R. Shippen commissioned the house at 1280 North Park Avenue as a "cottage" for his daughter, Zoe, and her husband, Dr. Eugene L. Jewett. This idiosyncratic Art Moderne–style house is an anomaly in the oeuvre of Rogers' residential projects, yet the house illustrates his capability as a designer of contemporary house styles. The Art Moderne style was popular in South Florida, as well as other areas during the 1930s, as streamlined industrial designs drew national attention. The house exhibits fundamental characteristics of the style in its use of glass block, curved corners, flat roofs, and asymmetrical facades. (See color plate 7)

Zoe Shippen, born in 1902 in Boston, was a noted artist, specializing in portrait painting. She had studied art at the École des Beaux-Arts Americaine at Fontainebleau, France, and at Boston's Museum School of Fine Arts. In the late 1920s she had residences in both Boston and Annisquam, Massachusetts, where George Noyes, another Rogers client, frequently summered. Zoe's portraits were the subject of several solo shows in New York, Florida, Rhode Island, Washington, and Cuba. Throughout the 1930s and 1940s her works were exhibited at shows in Winter Park that featured local artists.

Around 1936 Zoe married Dr. Eugene L. Jewett, an orthopedic surgeon. Born in 1900 in Fredonia, New York, Jewett graduated from

Cornell University with a bachelor of chemistry degree and then became a chemical engineer with the Barnett Corporation. In the fall of 1925, Jewett entered Harvard Medical College, after which the intern studied in Austria and in New York–area hospitals. In 1936, after one year as an associate in a private practice, Jewett opened his own orthopedic clinic in Orlando. Jewett gained international recognition for his invention of the hyper-extensive back brace and the hip nail, and for these advancements in his field, Jewett was named an honorary member of the American Academy of Orthopedic Surgeons. The orthopedic office that Jewett established is still in operation in Winter Park and Orlando.

When Eugene and Zoe Jewett's home on Lake Conway burned in 1937, Zoe's father, Dr. Shippen, commissioned Rogers to design a cottage for his daughter and son-in-law. The Shippens were still living in the Spanish Eclectic home that Rogers had designed for them in 1931, at 1290 North Park Avenue. The new house, which the Jewetts named "Tree Tops," would be located adjacent to the Shippens' own home within a small citrus grove on the south end of the property, which ran from the corner of New York and Park Avenues to Lake Maitland.[39]

The plan of the Jewett house is basically a compact pinwheel-type design—that is, the living spaces radiate outward from the center of the plan, which is occupied by a fireplace. The exterior image of the house is

Figure 13. Jewett house, second floor plan. By author. Courtesy of RLF.

a vertical mass with a flat roof. The most significant feature of the house is the two-story stair tower on the south facade, which is articulated by a vertical opening of glass block with a stepped surround. This prominent element provides a focal point for the house and permits ample light into the stairway. The entry to the house is on the west side of the stair tower and is sheltered by two projecting glass canopies with curved edges. Other stylistic features on the exterior include expanses of glass block that create curved corners on the second story, metal railings used along the roof terrace, and a metal circular stair on the east side of the house that led from a deck outside the second-story living room to the roof terrace, which was encircled in part by a concrete block parapet wall. The house was constructed of concrete block exterior walls that were painted white rather than finished with a coating of stucco.

The compact 1,200-square-foot house is arranged with the public spaces on the second floor and the utilitarian spaces on the ground floor,

Plate 49. Jewett house, upstairs living room. Photograph by Harold Haliday Costain. Courtesy of RLF.

a reversal of most traditional house plans. The ground floor contained a maid's room, a kitchen, a dining alcove, and a two-car garage, which was entered from the west side. The perfectly square stair hall, located immediately inside the entry door, led to the second floor, which consisted of a living room, bedroom, and study. The latter two spaces opened onto a screened porch, located on the west side of the house.

The interior decoration of the house bore the hand of its artistic owner. On the staircase Zoe stenciled black patterns onto white felt to simulate zebra skins. The walls of the living room were painted a cool dark gray, and there was a general absence of overt wood detailing. Zoe's portraits, including one of her husband, were hung throughout the house.

A particularly interesting feature in the living room is the fireplace mantelpiece, which has a stepped cornice with curved corners extending the entire length of the fireplace wall. This built-in detail augments the streamlined tenets of the Art Moderne style in the interior spaces.

The lack of trim work and the large areas of glass create a fluidity of space and evoke a sense of loftiness and also contribute to the stylistic continuation on the interior. An exposed steel pipe column supporting the roof allows for rounded glass block corners in the bedroom and living room. Earl Chabot, a general contractor based in Orlando, completed the construction of the Jewett house. This was a departure for Rogers, who had used Harry C. Cone on nearly all of his early projects.[40]

The Jewetts lived in Tree Tops for only four years. The couple soon divorced, and in the spring of 1941, the house was advertised as rental property.[41] After serving four years with the military in World War II, Dr. Jewett returned to Winter Park to continue his medical practice. In 1946 he commissioned Rogers to design another house for him, in Orlando at the corner of Glencoe and Fawsett Roads. Zoe Shippen eventually moved to Palm Beach.

In the Jewett house, as a result of the contemporary and artistic tastes of the owners, Rogers created an eccentric Art Moderne–style residence. He would never again design a building in this style, but the Leonard house, also designed in 1937, would present the architect with another challenge in a contemporary style.

Leonard House

1937

In 1937 Rogers designed a home for Mr. and Mrs. Edgar C. Leonard at 915 Old England Avenue. It was the only house Rogers designed in the International Style and may have been the first of its kind in the Central Florida area. Closely following the distinguishing characteristics of the style, the house consists of a two-story horizontal mass with a series of ribbon windows, asymmetrical facades, and a terrace located on the house's flat roof (pl. 50). In 1997 the house's exterior style was changed from sleek modernism to hybrid Mediterranean. While the structure of the house Rogers designed still exists, the image and elements used to create a Modern residence have been removed.

Edgar Cotrell Leonard was born in 1862 in Albany, New York. He attended Williams College, and in 1886, with his brother Gardener C. Leonard, he introduced the use of academic costume to his own graduation. Cotrell and Leonard, Inc., the firm founded by Leonard's grandfather in 1832, soon became the premiere supplier of caps and gowns for graduation and other ceremonies. Leonard, who became president of the firm, was active in the direction of the firm's retail stores and often

Plate 50. Leonard house, view to northwest. Photograph by Harold Haliday Costain. Courtesy of RLF.

made trips to Europe to obtain merchandise. Leonard married Bessie Woolworth, whose grandfather was the chancellor of New York University. After her death Leonard married Emily Nicoll of Westport, Connecticut, and Winter Park. Her father was James Craig Nicoll, a noted landscape artist of the late nineteenth and early twentieth centuries.[42]

Before commissioning Rogers to design a new home, the Leonards lived at 511 Osceola Avenue. The couple was often listed as guests at social functions around Winter Park, most notably at symphony events, since Leonard's younger sister, Dr. Mary L. Leonard, was a leading music patron and founder of the Symphony Orchestra of Central Florida. Leonard was also a trustee of Rollins College and had served as secretary of the Y.M.C.A. The Leonards' selection of Rogers as their architect was probably influenced by the publicity the architect had received locally over the previous few years. But Rogers had also known Leonard's nephew, Daniel Leonard, since his primary-school days in Winnetka. The two later attended Dartmouth College together.[43]

Throughout Rogers' career most of his work was based on historical models, such as the French Provincial, English Tudor, Colonial Revival, or Spanish house styles. In the Leonard house, however, the precedent for Rogers' design was a contemporary house designed in the International Style. The inspiration for this modern design came from Emily Leonard, who had seen a house in *Collier's* magazine designed by the noted American architect Edward Durell Stone. The house in *Collier's* was Stone's 1935 design for Richard H. Mandel in Mount Kisco, New York—a thoroughly modern design "executed in modern materials and furnished with the most recent equipment." Rogers was hesitant to replicate Stone's design without due credit, so he contacted Stone to discuss the design. In a show of professional courtesy, Rogers attributed the idea of the house design to Stone by crediting him in the title block of the Leonard house construction drawings.

Stone was a leading figure in the use of the International Style in residential design. The architect maintained that the Mandel house had been the "first modern house in the East," and he used the same design elements in his house for Conger Goodyear on Long Island and Ulrich Kowalski in Mount Kisco.[44] Defining features of all three houses were the use of concrete and steel construction, flat roofs, strip or ribbon windows, and glass block. Rogers utilized these stylistic elements in his design for the Leonard house, but he combined them with practical adaptations to the Florida environment and to the specific site conditions.

The Leonard house was sited on a large wooded lot with a small citrus grove. While the majority of houses along Old England Avenue were arranged with their main facades fronting the avenue, the Leonard house turned an austere, narrow side facade to the street. The house was further obscured by the presence of a garden wall. This peculiar arrangement, however, provided a private and serene view of the landscape to the south from inside the house. Because of its orientation on the property, which actually incorporated two lots totaling nearly an acre, the house had the feel of being located on a much larger estate.

The structural system Rogers employed in the Leonard house is unusual for residential construction of the time. It is a combination of load-bearing concrete block walls and steel pipe columns, upon which rest steel beams, open web steel joists, and wooden beams. The steel beams span the width of the living room and are cantilevered beyond this space to support the roof deck above. The open web steel joists span between the steel beams and are covered with metal decking and con-

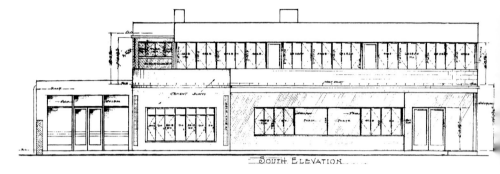

Figure 14. Leonard house, south elevation. Courtesy of RLF.

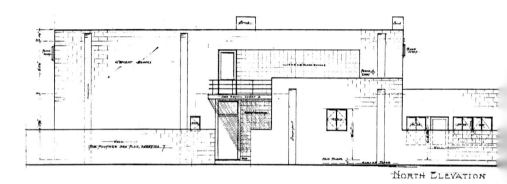

Figure 15. Leonard house, north elevation. Courtesy of RLF.

crete to provide a first floor ceiling assembly. The wood beams are used to support the second-story roof.

Overall, the Leonard house presented a strong horizontal image, with north and south facades more than seventy feet long. The continuous strip of ribbon windows, metal railings, and flat roofs further emphasized the house's length. The entrance, located off center on the north facade, was placed well away from the street. While understated, the entrance featured a flanking wall of glass block on both the first and second floors. A cantilevered concrete deck on the second floor, which also served as a canopy over the door, had curved corners and was encircled by metal railings, typical of the International Style. The house's basic rectangular shape was broken on the south facade by the projecting half-round form of the dining room. The rounded wall held numerous windows that provided a view of the south lawn from the interior. In fact, with a continuous strip of windows across it, the south facade was basically a wall of glass that opened onto the lawn and grove.

The Leonard house consisted of two stories, with a full-height basement located directly under the entry foyer and kitchen. The large fifteen-by-twenty-eight-foot living room was the dominant space on the first floor of the house and incorporated a nine-foot ceiling. The south wall of the room was composed of a continuous strip of ribbon windows, which were partially shaded by an overhanging roof deck on the second floor. A terrace on the south side of the house, which was separated from the street by an expanse of lawn and a five-foot-tall concrete block wall, was accessed through a door on the east wall of the living room. Other spaces on the first floor included the kitchen and pantry at the far west end of the house, with a breakfast terrace beyond; a guest bedroom with bath; and the semicircular dining room, which gave the south facade its distinct exterior form.

The stairs Rogers designed for the Leonard house were unlike any he had completed previously and were a particularly artistic expression of space. Located west of the entry, the stairs incorporated a modernistic

Plate 52. Leonard house, stair column and light fixture. Photograph by author.

central column that rose full height through the stair hall. The column stopped short of the ceiling and was capped by a lighting fixture consisting of a flat disk of Carrara glass and luster glass. The entire north wall of the stairs was punctuated with an expanse of glass block, which gave the space a luminous quality through bright, indirect natural lighting. The lower section of the staircase was shaped in a semicircle and evoked a feeling of motion as the stairs spiraled up to the second floor.

The second floor of the Leonard house consisted of three bedrooms, two baths, and a roof deck that stretched along the entire length of the house. The roof deck provided a pleasant, open space to enjoy the views of the garden, while the screened porch at the southwest corner was a semi-enclosed space that was used as a sleeping porch.

The Leonards lived in the house for only a few years. Mr. Leonard died in 1938, one year after the house was completed, and Mrs. Leonard remained in the house three more years, until 1941. In the 1950s Elsa Borden and her husband, Gail, whose grandfather founded the Borden

Dairy Company in New York, moved into the house with their two young daughters. Gail Borden died in 1991, and in 1995 Elsa sold the house. The new owners, desiring a Mediterranean image for the house, clad the exterior with heavily textured stucco, replaced the flat roofs with gable roofs clad with terra-cotta barrel tiles, changed the windows, and reoriented the entrance. They retained one relic from Rogers' design: a curving corner of glass block near the kitchen.

The Leonard house was an extremely important building in the career of James Gamble Rogers II. Together with the Jewett house, it represents Rogers' ability to produce well-organized, well-detailed contemporary architecture in response to the varied tastes of his clients.

Burress House

1939

Nearly ten years after completing his own French Provincial home on the Isle of Sicily, Gamble Rogers was commissioned to build the second home on the island, for Mr. and Mrs. Paul Burress. Though his own house had resulted in much publicity for the young architect, it did not attract many homeowners to the island as the developers had hoped. A decade after its creation, though, the Isle of Sicily began to draw the attention of Winter Park residents, and today it is one of the most desirable addresses in the city. (See color plate 8.)

The Burress house was designed in the Tudor Revival style, which, although popular in other parts of the country, was fairly uncommon in Florida. The popularity of the style in America can be traced back to the Queen Anne style that often precisely followed English precedents. In the Tudor style, on the other hand, designers choose freely from medieval prototypes, often combining folk elements with formal elements. Rogers had designed only one house in this style, the John N. Huttig house (1934) on Lake Conway in Orlando, which was completed for Rogers' cousin Laura Randall and her husband. Both the Huttig and Burress houses employ typical attributes of the style, such as ornamental half-timbering, steeply pitched roofs, casement and bay windows, and elaborately detailed chimneys.

The address of the triangular lot the Burresses purchased was 1 Isle of Sicily, which is located to the south as one crosses the Isle of Sicily bridge. Like all lots on the island, the site had expansive views of Lake Maitland to the south and west and was sufficiently wide enough to provide a lawn on both the street side and lakeside.

The balanced scheme of the front facade features a deeply recessed, paneled entry door located off center, three gable-roofed wall dormers that pierce the eave of the side-facing gable roof, and half-timbering on the second-floor level. A one-story front-gable wing, which projects from the main wall plane, features half-timbering and horizontal cypress siding with bark edges in the gable end. To the west, a heavy timber loggia leads to the separate garage, which later was enlarged with a second story.

The exterior materials Rogers used in the design of the Burress house evoke a warm, textured quality. The roofs are covered with flat terracotta tiles. The house was of frame construction clad with a combination of brick veneer and ornamental half-timbering of dark heavy timber members infilled with stucco. With the exception of the north facade of the kitchen, the first story is clad with brick that was painted white. The second story and the kitchen facade are clad with half-timbering. The contrast of the dark wood and the terra-cotta roof tiles against the white of the stucco and painted brick gives the house its distinctive Tudor appearance. The overall effect of the rustic materials, historical design, and overhanging live oak trees and Spanish moss is of a storybook scene.

The lakeside facade of the Burress house is dominated by the projecting wing of the living room, which features a bay window with a copper roof, cypress siding in the gable end, and a large stucco and brick chimney topped with a decorative metal cap. While some half-timbering is present on this facade, Rogers chose to intensify the contrast of the white painted brick of the first story by cladding the second story with the same dark siding used in the gable ends of the kitchen wing and the living room. (See color plate 9.)

Entering the Burress house, a visitor experiences a sequence of spaces similar to that found in Rogers' Holt house of 1937 (fig. 16). Because of the difference in architectural style, the details naturally differ between the Burress and Holt houses, but in both the main entry sets the stage for the dramatic sequence of spaces that follows. The Burress foyer is aligned through a pointed-arch opening with the double-height living room beyond. As one enters the living room, a U-shaped staircase, located to the right, leads to a balcony overlooking the room from the second floor. The living room is articulated with exposed four-by-six-inch hand-hewn rafters and collar beams. This dynamic arrangement of spaces is extended visually into the landscape beyond the house by a large bay window at the south end of the living room that looks out onto

Plate 53. Burress house, detail of half-timbering above entrance. Photograph by author.

Lake Maitland. (See color plate 10.) Other spaces located on the first floor include a master bedroom and screened porch on the east side and a dining room and kitchen on the west side.

The curving staircase leads to the balcony on the second floor, from which a hall extends to a perpendicular passage. A guest room is located at the east end of the passage, and a maid's room at the west.

A garage and studio are located west of the main house and are connected to the house by a loggia and enclosed hallway above. The studio is a particularly cozy space that was used by the Burresses as an office. It is richly appointed, with a stone fireplace, oak floor, and plaster ceiling. Plaster was also specified on the construction drawings as an interior wall finish. Presently, however, the walls are covered with magnolia wood paneling, which lends a distinctive, warm feel to the sixteen-foot-square room.

Several additions and alterations have been made to the Burress house, but all have been in harmony with the original design. In 1950

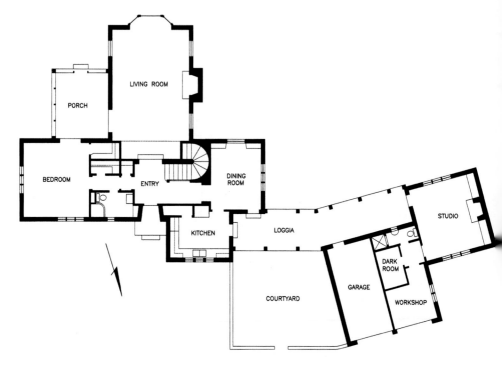

Figure 16. Burress house, first floor plan. By author. Courtesy of RLF.

the fifth and current owners of the house, Mr. and Mrs. John Tiedtke, commissioned Rogers to lengthen and add a second story to the existing garage and to eliminate the original workshop and darkroom spaces, formerly in the west bay, to create space for a second car. In the 1980s Rogers' firm also added an elevator tower and vestibule to the west end of the house.

The Burress house was a welcome addition to the Isle of Sicily. After ten years of solitary habitation of the island, the Rogerses finally would have neighbors. Furthermore, the Tudor Revival style of the Burress house would complement the French Provincial style of Rogers' own cottage. Both styles featured a variety of exterior materials and a variety of forms and distinctive architectural elements. Located at the entrance to the island, the Burress house gives visitors the initial impression of crossing into another time and place.

Plant House

1939

In April 1939 Mrs. Caroline Griggs Plant of Cohasset, Massachusetts, purchased the property of E. Kellogg Trowbridge, located between Palmer Avenue and Lake Osceola.[45] Mrs. Plant then commissioned Gamble Rogers to design a large Spanish Eclectic house. Mrs. Plant's father was a pioneer publisher of Chicago and Illinois history. Her homes in both Cohasset, just outside of Boston, and Chicago were described in a newspaper article as "palatial" showplaces that were frequently open for philanthropic purposes.[46]

The Plant house is a two-story stucco-clad house with a side-facing gable roof over the central section. In the organization of spaces and overall scale, the Plant house resembles Rogers' earlier design for the Barbour house. At nearly 7,000 square feet, however, the Plant house is larger than the Barbour house and, indeed, is the largest residence Rogers ever designed. It has a rambling appearance, which is not surprising given that the east-to-west facade of the house is more than 125 feet long and covers the building lot nearly edge to edge. (See color plate 11.)

Rogers, however, handled this expansive facade well, by varying roof heights, by using gable and cross gable roofs to define separate elements, and by varying window types and carefully placing window and door openings. The roofs were covered with terra-cotta barrel tiles. The windows, which were largely single and double casements, were varied through the use of concrete and wrought-iron grilles, stucco surrounds, and even a cast stone oriel with an arched bottle-end-glass window. The projecting kitchen wing on the east end of the facade was enhanced by an arched, corbelled string course. These materials and elements added dimension, texture, and variety to the facade.

On the lakeside facade, Rogers used a proliferation of window and door openings, rather than applied ornament, to vary the house's appearance. Every room on this side of the house had visual access from the interior to the courtyard and lake. On the second story a heavy timber balcony and a deck provided additional spatial relief along the facade.

The outdoor living spaces of the loggia, terrace, and courtyard occupied much of the land between the house and lake (fig 17). The loggia had a tile floor, while the terrace was paved with concrete and the open-air courtyard with flagstones. A quatrefoil fountain was placed in the center of the courtyard, surrounded by built-in planting boxes on all sides. An exterior stair on the east wall of the courtyard led to the deck on the roof of the breakfast room. Rogers detailed this stair with the familiar underside arch previously used at the Barbour house in the interior courtyard stair and at the Barbour Apartments. With its many balconies, terraces, planters, and stepped retaining walls, the Plant house gives the impression of spilling over its lot into the lake.

As at the Barbour house, one enters the Plant house via a centrally located doorway, which is highly decorated with a trefoil arch, cast stone double chevron surrounds, and stucco quoining. The slightly projecting bay of the entry is covered with a tiled gable roof. A wooden screen door of split spindles covered the elaborate paneled front door. The doorway arch is reminiscent of the one Rogers used at the Ingram house, and is more Venetian or more broadly Mediterranean than authentically Spanish.

The initial series of interior spaces is unusual for a residence and more closely resembles a hotel or theater entry in that a lobby is provided, which is flanked by a coat room and a powder room. Stepping up from the lobby, one then enters a large entrance hall nearly forty-five feet in length. Triple arched openings on the south wall of the hall—with a fixed window in the center and double-leaf, multipane doors on the sides—lead to the loggia and then the sunken patio with Lake Osceola beyond.

At the west end of the hall, visitors could await their host in the reception room, which opened on the south side to the formal living room. The opening was detailed with plaster ogee arches supported by twisted columns and pilasters. (See color plate 12.) A difference in floor levels, a result of the sloping terrain of the building lot, necessitated two steps down into the living room, which was finished with tile floors and a ceiling of applied wooden molding intended to simulate ornate coffered panels. The room held a large fireplace on the east wall and several built-in bookshelves and cabinets. An ornamental iron gate at the southwest corner of the space opened onto an enclosed porch, which was octagonal in shape.

The formal dining room was located southeast of the entrance hall and featured false wood beams in the plaster ceiling. The space continued south into the breakfast room, which was several steps below the dining room. The opening into the breakfast room was detailed with a railing featuring twisted wrought-iron newels and spindles. The breakfast room was brightly lit with windows on all sides and a door leading into the courtyard on the west. Both dining areas were equipped with a floor button that rang directly to the wait staff in the kitchen.

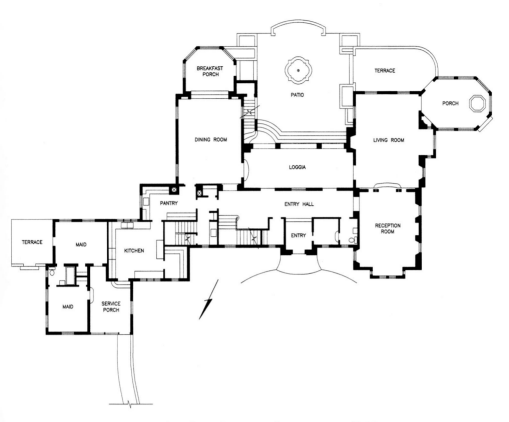

Figure 17. Plant house, first floor plan. By author. Courtesy of RLF.

The extensive service wing was located on the east end of the house and provided quarters for two, a kitchen, a pantry, a screened service porch, and a private stair to the second floor.

The owners' stairs were placed in the northeast corner of the entrance hall and featured a short rise before turning at a landing and returning to the west. The fixed-sash windows above the landing held leaded panes of bottle-end glass within a trefoil arched opening. Ornate wrought-iron railings and balusters lined the staircase, and a velvet-covered handrail was provided on the interior wall.

The rooms on the second floor of the Plant house were arranged around a central hall that ran the length of the house. Each of the three bedrooms was equipped with a bath and two or more walk-in closets. The bedroom at the southwest corner opened to a heavy timber balcony on the south and to a sitting room and office on the southeast. The bedroom located above the dining room opened on the south to an open roof deck. A sewing room was located above the first-floor reception room. Maid's quarters, cedar-lined storage closets, and other storage spaces were located in the northeast corner of the second floor.

The interior walls of the Plant house were plaster, although their surfaces were varied with small alcoves, niches, and built-in shelves and cabinets. The floors in the reception room, the dining room, the breakfast room, and the bedrooms were of oak, while those in the entrance hall and the living room were tile.

A separate two-car garage with a porte cochere and a laundry building were located on the eastern edge of the property and were connected to the service portion of the main house by a concrete walkway. A cupola with a standing-seam copper roof and wooden louvers topped the garage building, which was delineated in the same style and materials as the main house. The garage was equipped with an overhead car-washing mechanism.

Caroline Griggs Plant died in 1947 and directed her executors, among them Ray Greene, to sell all her personal property, furnishings, and effects, including her home in Winter Park. The money was to be disbursed to a wide array of philanthropic institutions, including Rollins College, the Boston Museum of Fine Arts, and All Saints Episcopal Church. Mrs. Plant also directed that all her private papers and photographs be burned "without perusal."[47]

The Plant house design contained the largest amount of applied ornament and interior detailing of any house Rogers had completed to this point in his career. Clearly, the client required elaborate entertaining spaces in addition to well-furnished private rooms. While primarily Spanish Eclectic in style, the house borrows from other Mediterranean vocabularies in its ornamental program. Rogers' manipulation of forms alleviates the impact such an enormous house might have on the site and provides a pleasing addition to the lakeshore, both to the casual observer and to the inhabitants.

Mizener House

1939

The architectural style that Rogers worked in as much as, and perhaps more than, the Spanish Eclectic style was the Colonial Revival style, which was eminently popular during the early twentieth century and continues as one of American homeowners' favorite styles. In fact, after the Barbour house, Rogers is probably best known for his design of the

Colonial Revival–style Mizener house, which was completed in 1939. (See color plate 13.)

The National Centennial in 1876 is often cited as the seminal event in rekindling America's interest in the colonial period, especially its architectural character. Professional publications such as *The Georgian Period*, published by the *American Architect and Building News*, and *Architectural Forum*'s *White Pine Series of Architectural Monographs* provided practicing architects and builders with measured drawings, photographs, and authentic details of regionally important colonial buildings, both from the South and from the New England colonies. Soon, the style became more widely disseminated across the country through such magazines as *Ladies Home Journal*, *Better Homes and Gardens*, and *House Beautiful*. The 1930s reconstruction of the colonial structures in Williamsburg, Virginia, further enhanced the appeal of the style.[48]

As with other revival styles, the majority of Colonial Revival work was a free interpretation and blending of elements from colonial-era precedents. Small frame or brick houses might exhibit influences of the style in the use of a gooseneck pediment above the front door, double-hung sash windows, or an elaborate cornice.

For Rogers, adapting the Colonial Revival style to the Florida climate meant that most of his work would be of frame construction rather than brick. Prior to World War II, Rogers' Colonial Revival–style houses were usually two stories; were sometimes clad with wooden shingles; featured detailed entrances with pilasters, columns, or pedimented doorways; and were the result of the client's specific request for a home designed in the style. A few prewar designs were story-and-a-half Cape Cod–style frame houses. After the war Rogers' Colonial Revival–style houses were much more modest, often only one story with a minimum of detailing. Construction of the houses also changed from frame to concrete masonry, which during the 1950s became the most popular construction method in Florida for its ease and durability in the brutal climate.

In 1936 Mildred Wells Mizener, widow of Frank Mizener, approached Rogers about designing a house for the large lot she had purchased on Lake Maitland, fronting onto Palmer Avenue and just across from the Schmidt house, which Rogers had designed in 1935. Mrs. Mizener had come to Winter Park in 1929 from North East, Pennsylvania. She was a member of the First Church of Christ Scientist, for which Rogers would design a new sanctuary and educational building in 1958. In 1938

Rogers had designed a home for Mr. and Mrs. Charles O. Andrews Jr., Mrs. Mizener's daughter and son-in-law.

Rogers recalled his client as being "very shrewd" with her money, and though she wanted a "Southern Colonial house," she did not want what Rogers called "characteristic adornments" such as shutters because she did not want to paint them every year. Maintaining the integrity of the colonial design was paramount to Rogers and his design team, which was headed by Laurance Hitt. Mrs. Mizener was quite adamant about deleting items that she felt "weren't structurally necessary or aesthetically essential," and she would pencil out such elements as she reviewed preliminary drawings for the house. This, of course, did not sit well with the architectural professionals, and Hitt, in particular, became somewhat frustrated with the client's insistence on changing the design.

Rogers remembered that one of Mrs. Mizener's "check lists" bothered Hitt more than usual, and he began to annotate the list with his own comments such as "this won't work"; "this is a silly idea"; "she's going to ruin this house"; and "dammit, NO." The comments lay benignly in the project file until one day when Mrs. Mizener visited the Rogers office and asked the secretary if she might see the file. Undoubtedly, the client saw the designer's comments on the previous check list. Several days later, Mrs. Mizener returned to review yet another check list with Hitt. Rogers recalled, "When they were through, she started for the door, but stopped and said 'Oh, I forgot something.' She came back to Laurance's table and at the bottom of her list of notes wrote 'Oh Hell!'"[49]

The Mizener house is situated on the north end of a large lot prominently located at the intersection of Georgia and Palmer Avenues and overlooking Lake Maitland to the north. The location of the house and the fact that passersby have an unencumbered view of the house across an open lawn have led to its local fame as a Rogers design. The house has historically been painted white, which adds to the plantation feel of the property.

The house was constructed of standard concrete block with a finish coat of stucco. Windows are double-hung sash featuring both six-over-nine and six-over-six panes. The large central section of the house, which is covered with a single hipped roof pierced by splayed dormers with rounded roofs, is flanked on the west by a two-story wing and on the east by a one-story porte cochere, from which one entered into the library rather than a separate entry hall. The lakefront facade is distin-

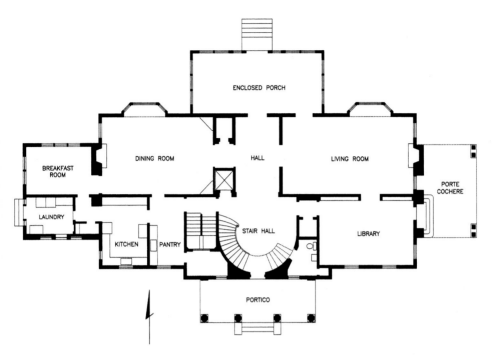

Figure 18. Mizener house, first floor plan. By author. Courtesy of RLF.

guished by projecting bay windows in the living room and dining room, between which was a one-story enclosed porch. This space was detailed with Tuscan pilasters and pairs of double hung windows.

The Neo-Classically inspired, double-height portico supported by four elongated Tuscan columns dominates the street-side facade of the Mizener house. Though essential to the Colonial Revival image of the house, the original columns appeared too slender for the proportions of the portico and house—an unusual miscalculation in a Rogers design. Recently, the original columns were replaced by more correctly proportional fluted columns with Ionic capitals. The pediment features a ribbon-adorned carved wooden cartouche depicting a shield, which contained a fixed-sash window. The centrally located entrance is within a projecting three-bay-wide form, which features stucco quoins on the sides. Fluted pilasters flank the entrance, and a broken pediment tops the doorway; a Palladian window is located on the second story, above the door.

Like the Plant house, the Mizener house exhibits a plan that was designed for entertaining on a grand scale. Service areas, including the kitchen and pantry, are compacted into the southwest corner of the first floor and are separated from the public spaces by a series of doors. This area has a separate exterior entry on the west side of the house.

One enters the house beneath the grand circular stair that rises through the center of the double-height stair hall, an arrangement that recalls the Neo-Georgian–style architecture of the American colonial period. The stair hall, a space that is nearly eighteen feet square and rises in the center to a height of twenty feet, serves as the primary receiving area and leads into a ten-foot-wide center hallway to the north. Rogers used the spaces beneath the stairs to tuck in a half bath, a large storage space with laundry chute to the basement level, and a coat closet. Rogers had used the same design, albeit on a smaller scale, for a similar space in the earlier Walter H. Tappan house, though this use of all available space might have been prompted by Mrs. Mizener's frugality. (See color plate 14.)

Central to the Mizener house design are the balance and symmetry of the plan. The arrangement of entrance, stair hall, center hall, and an enclosed porch beyond is the main south-to-north axis through the house. The main east-to-west axis runs from the east wall of the living room, through the center hall, and into the dining room. A library, located at the southeast corner of the house, provides a more intimate space for guests.

The public spaces on the first floor were generously proportioned, with ten-foot ceilings, and the layout provided numerous circulation routes. The library, a moderately sized space of twenty-two by fifteen feet, contains pine paneling above bookshelves that, despite the room's intended purpose, were to be located solely on the north wall of the room. The remaining walls were to be plastered. The living room, an impressive thirty by seventeen feet, is located north of the library and contains an elaborately carved fireplace, with a marble hearth, on the east wall. A bay window with a built-in window seat, which looks out onto Lake Maitland, is centrally located on the north side of the room.

Passing west through the center hall, one enters the dining room, also large at twenty-five and a half by seventeen feet. China cabinets were built into the northeast and southeast corners of the room, and a bay window with a built-in window seat, matching that of the living room, was centrally located on the north wall. A marble-fronted fireplace with a bolection molding surround and a raised panel above is located on the west wall of the dining room, balancing the design with the living room. Doors located south of the fireplace lead to the breakfast room, which composes the first floor of the west wing of the house.

The breakfast room, cozy by comparison at fifteen feet wide by eight and a half feet deep, had windows on the west and north walls and a service door to the kitchen on the south.

The second story of the Mizener house, accessed by the dramatically curving center stair, contained four bedrooms, four full baths, a sewing room, and several closets and storage spaces. Mrs. Mizener's suite was located on the second floor of the west wing.

An enclosed service stair, located west of the ceremonial central stairs, enabled undetected movement through the house by domestic workers. These stairs are the only access to the partial basement of the house, which contained a furnace room, laundry, half bath, and finished room that may have served as maid's quarters.

Harry Cone was the general contractor for the Mizener project, and local master painter Alvin A. Marriott, who had arrived in Winter Park at about the same time as Rogers and had completed work for local architects Harold Hare and Maurice Kressly, was selected for painting and decorating the house. J. O. Youtsey and Co., also a local company, completed the plaster and extensive stucco work. The construction of the house was completed for $35,000.

Though a Laurance Hitt rendering of the Mizener house was published in the 1940 issue of *Florida Architecture and Allied Arts*, the house was not, according to Rogers' son, one of his father's favorite designs. It may have been that the difficult architect-client relationship left a lingering distaste for the job, and that the architect did not quite get the design he wanted for the house because of the client's personal choices. Interestingly, during his later years Rogers cited his 1937 Colonial Revival–style house for R. D. (Dolf) Keene, on Lake Adair in Orlando, as one of his personal favorites—a house that is quite similar to the Mizener house (pl. 54).[50]

As with the Mizener house, Rogers used his favorite general contractor, Harry Cone, on the Keene job, and Alvin Marriott was again called upon for painting and decorating. George Camp Keiser in Orlando was the associated architect. The house is similar to the Mizener house in its use of the Neo-Classical portico, its massing, and its overall form, though the Keene house is covered by a gable roof rather than a hipped roof. The Keene house was featured in the 1939 issue of *Florida Architecture and Allied Arts*.

The Keene and Mizener houses were two of the last residential projects Rogers completed before the onset of World War II. Though Rogers would complete a number of residential designs after the war, he would be known primarily for his prewar designs, which continue to beautify Winter Park's neighborhoods.

Appendix. Catalogue of Residential Work

The following catalogue of James Gamble Rogers II's residential work was compiled from existing drawings, newspaper articles, and other published accounts. Often the drawings were not labeled with the proposed building address. In these cases we have researched the Orlando–Winter Park directories in an attempt to determine the addresses of the houses designed by Rogers. We made site visits in an effort to confirm these assumptions, but historical buildings had often been replaced by modern structures. In some cases an existing building bore no semblance to the drawings, leading us to assume that the historical building had been severely altered, that the project had never been built, or that the address derived from the city directories was inaccurate. All of the above situations are noted in the catalogue, with brackets around an

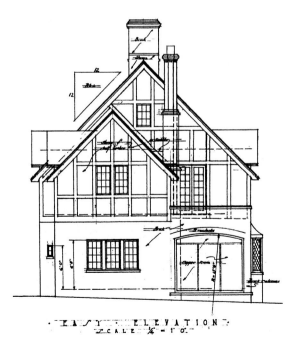

· EAST ELEVATION ·
SCALE ¼" = 1' 0".

Fig. 19. Huttig house, east elevation. Courtesy of RLF.

assumed address. Some drawings were undated, in which cases we have so indicated (n.d.) or have made an attempt to date the drawings by correlation with other designs or information.

D. B. Alexander
Residence
Peninsula Drive
Daytona Beach, 1949

W. J. Alford
Residence
1321 Fairview Avenue
Winter Park, 1952

F. Monroe Alleman
Residence
1723 Spring Lake Drive
Orlando, 1962

B. G. Anderson
Residence
Eustis, 1948

Martin Anderson
Studies for residence
Orlando, 1951

Charles O. Andrews
Residence
Winter Park, 1938

Mrs. William Arnett
Alterations to residence
Clermont, 1948

Barbour Apartments
Multifamily units
Knowles and Swoope Avenues
Winter Park, 1938

Robert Bruce Barbour
Residence
Casa Feliz
656 North Interlachen Avenue
Now located on North Park Avenue
Winter Park, 1932

H. W. Barnum
Residence
201 Genius Drive
Winter Park, 1947

W. Leonard Bartlum
Residence
1611 Spring Lake Drive
Orlando, 1940

Millicent Bertram
Cottage
1404 Elm Avenue
Winter Park, 1949

Doris Bingham
Residence
160 Glenridge Way
Winter Park, 1937

L. V. Bledsoe
Residence—demolished
486 Virginia Court
Winter Park, 1941

H. Bourne
Alterations to residence
[423 Palmer Avenue?]
Orlando, n.d.

U. T. Bradley
Residence
1243 Alberta Drive
Winter Park, 1936
Alterations, 1940

William Bradner
Lakeside cottage
Crystal Lake, n.d.

Doris Bingham
Residence

U. T. Bradley
Residence

Louis H. Brereton
Residence
[960 Keyes Avenue?]
[420 Sylvan Drive?]
Winter Park, 1952

General Brett
Residence
Orlando, 1946

Brewer Estate
Alterations to The Palms
(now known as
  Trismen Terrace)
Winter Park, 1937

Mrs. A. L. Bridgers
Residence
Altamonte Springs, 1951

Ervin Theodore Brown
Residence
250 Virginia Drive
Winter Park, 1939

Ervin Theodore Brown
Residence

Mrs. William E. Casselberry Residence

Henry Bruere
Residence
890 Georgia Avenue
Winter Park, 1953

Roy Bunn
Mountain cabin
North Carolina, 1947

Alice D. Burnett
Alterations to garage apartment
1176 Via Capri
Winter Park, 1939

Paul Burress
Residence
1 Isle of Sicily
Winter Park, 1939

Archibald Granville Bush
Residence
1200 North Park Avenue
Winter Park, 1949

William Canole
Residence
Orlando, 1972

Victor N. Camp
Residence
Seton Trail
Ormond Beach, 1926

A. R. Carver
Residence
Lakeland, 1940

Hibbard Casselberry
Residence
Casselberry, 1952

Mrs. William E. Casselberry
Residence (cottage)
Fern Park, 1937

Mrs. William E. Casselberry
Guest house
Casselberry, 1952

Mrs. William E. Casselberry
Residence
2131 Via Tuscany
(now the Winter Park Racquet Club)
Winter Park, n.d.

Casselberry
Alterations and additions
Lake Triplet Drive
Winter Park, 1969

Mel [Mrs. William] Casselberry
Residence
Blowing Rock, N.C., 1947

S. O. Chase
Residence
Sanford, 1954

George L. Chindal
Residence
900 South Lake Sybelia Drive
Maitland, 1936

Dr. Lucius C. Clark
Residence
325 Victoria Avenue
Winter Park, 1934

R. A. Clark
Alterations to residence
Winter Haven, 1946

Claude
Residence
Winter Park, 1946

N. T. Cobb Jr.
Residence
Merritt Island, n.d.

Clarence A. Coddington
Residence
800 Palmer Avenue
Winter Park, 1941

Eugene D. Coleman
Residence
366 Alberta Drive
Winter Park, 1948

Dr. Lucius C. Clark
Residence

Eugene D. Coleman
Studio—demolished
(366 Alberta Drive)
Winter Park, 1940

Vernon L. Conner
Residence
Lake Gem
Mount Dora, 1951

Samuel S. Conover
Alterations to residence
Ormond Beach, n.d.

William A. Craig
Residence, boathouse
1511 Via Tuscany
Winter Park, 1948

Robert F. Crane
Residence
176 Gaines Way
Winter Park, 1957

George R. Crisler
Residence
251 Courtland Street
Winter Park, n.d.

Wilbur J. Croxton
Residence
Mount Dora, 1949

Wilbur J. Croxton
Residence
Tavares, 1949

Blair Culpepper
Residence
Clearwater, 1982

S. J. Davies
Residence
2080 Via Lugano
Winter Park, 1951

John Davis
Alterations to residence
Eustis, n.d.

Nelson S. Dearmont
Residence
Winter Park, 1948

Dehoyos
Alterations to residence
1000 Old England Avenue
Winter Park, [1980?]

Eric DeLaMater
Study for residence
Daytona Beach, 1947

Mrs. Melville Dewey
Residence
301 Interlachen Avenue
Winter Park, 1939

Mrs. J. W. Dillenback
Alterations to residence
Daytona, n.d.

Robert Doherty
Residence
North Park Avenue
Winter Park, 1949

Robert Doherty
Residence
Daytona Beach, 1950

J. P. Drane
Residence
Sebring, 1948

Allan Duke (Lucy Masek)
Residence
[801 Elizabeth Drive?]
Winter Park, [1950?]

Commander L. H. Dyer
Alterations to residence
1428 Lake Knowles Circle
Winter Park, 1937

Grace O. Edwards
Residence

Oliver K. Eaton
Alterations to residence
1420 Via Tuscany
Winter Park, 1946

David Edgerton
Alterations to residence
Mount Dora, 1940

Grace O. Edwards
Residence
425 Alberta Drive
Winter Park, 1935

O. Raymond Ellars
Residence
[1247 East Livingston Avenue, 1941?]
[Waterwitch Drive, 1951?]
Orlando, n.d.

Harold H. Elliott
Residence—demolished
(1234 Palmer Avenue)
Winter Park, 1950

Wooda B. Elliott
Porch addition
914 Lincoln Circle
Winter Park, 1962

E. J. Elting
Residence
Mount Dora, 1951

Thomas Elwyn
Alterations to residence
Tallahassee, 1948

T. E. Emery
Residence
1135 Lakeview Drive
Winter Park, 1945

H. J. Emptage
Apartment building
Winter Park, 1946

G. C. Erie
Alterations and additions
Maitland, 1952

Norman F. Fain Jr.
Residence
Eau Gaullie, La., 1971

R. F. Fertig
Residence
850 Osceola Avenue
Winter Park, 1940

B. Allison Galloway
Residence
Lake Howell
Winter Park, 1949

Mrs. Stanley Galpin
Studies for residence
Southport, Conn., 1937

Claude Gary Jr.
Residence
125 Hampton Circle
Winter Park, 1939

Jack George
Studies for residence
Cocoa, 1938

Leroy Giles
Residence
539 Delaney
Orland, 1941

W. F. Gillies
Residence
[208 East Morse Avenue #3?]
Winter Park, 1948

James Goodwin
Alterations to residence
[600 Maiden Lane, James H.]
[1631 Alabama, James L.]
Winter Park, 1955

C. H. Grasser
Residence
Highland Park, 1956

Ray Greene
Garage apartment
242 Chase Avenue
Winter Park, 1951

Stephen Gregor
Residence
Mount Dora, 1947

Charles C. Gressange
Residence
1515 Harmon Avenue
Winter Park, 1947

A. H. Gunn
Alterations to residence—
    demolished
(506 New York Avenue)
Winter Park, n.d.

J. Thomas Gurney
Residence
1701 Spring Lake Road
Orlando, 1953

Joseph S. Guernsey
Studies for residence
Orlando, 1962

Lomax Gwathmey
Residence
Orange County, 1938

Noble Hall
Residence
Fern Park, ca. 1930

Fred Hall
Residence
664 Osceola Avenue
Winter Park, 1939

Fred L. Hall
Apartment/duplex
Lyman Avenue
Winter Park, 1947

Herbert Halverstadt
Apartment building
Winter Park, 1947

Huron M. Hamilton
Residence
1161 Palmer Avenue
Winter Park, 1950

Mrs. Hannum
Beach house
Daytona, 1940

Percival Harris
Residence—unbuilt
Winter Park, ca. 1936

Eldridge Hart
Residence
[408 East Lyman Avenue? 1935]
[422 Lyman Avenue? 1933]
Winter Park, n.d.

E. E. Haskell
Residence
Clermont, 1951

L. S. Haslam
Normandy Road
Casselberry, ca. 1930

Frederick A. Hauck
Residence
2 Isle of Sicily
Winter Park, 1946

Joseph C. Hayward
Residence
Virginia Avenue
Orlando, 1951

K. H. Hill
Residence
1615 South Mills
Orlando, 1938

L. G. Hoffman
Residence
Palmer Avenue
Winter Park, 1951

Roger Holler
Residence
1301 Alberta Drive
Winter Park, 1975

W. E. Holler
Residence
Mount Dora, 1950

George C. Holt
Residence
1430 Elizabeth Drive
Winter Park, 1937
Alterations and additions, 1941

R. F. Hotard
Alterations to residence
1420 Elizabeth Drive (altered)
Winter Park, 1955

Percival S. Howard
Residence
1031 Osceola Avenue
Winter Park, 1948

Robert M. Howard
Residence
1 Waverly Place
Orlando, 1938

Robert M. Howard
Residence
Annie Street and Lake Copeland
Orlando, 1935

House at Dubsdread
1941

Mrs. Charles G. Humphreys
Alterations to residence
1759 Alabama Drive
The Rambles
Winter Park, 1947

John N. Huttig
Residence
435 Peachtree Road
Orlando, 1934
(in association with David B. Hyer,
   architect)

Douglas Igou
Residence
Eustis, 1950

L. C. Ingram
Residence
842 Laurel Street
Orlando, 1935

Louis W. Ingram
Porch addition
907 Old England Avenue
Winter Park, 1953

Anna Jenks
Alterations to residence
160 Overlook Road
Winter Park, 1940

Eugene L. Jewett
Residence
Fawcett and Glencoe Roads
Winter Park, 1946

A. C. Johnson
Residence
Mount Dora, 1930
Additions, 1950

Walter B. Johnston
Alterations to residence
1401 Grove Terrace
Winter Park, 1946

Kauffman
Alterations to residence
Grand Island, 1939

R. D. Keene
Residence
1030 Lake Adair Boulevard
Orlando, 1937

R. D. Keene
Residence for daughter, Mrs. Robert
   Crane
Tallahassee, 1948

N. Kennedy
Alterations to residence
440 Sylvan Drive
Winter Park, 1951

John N. Huttig
Residence

*R. D. Keene
Residence*

E. G. Kilroe
Alterations and additions—
  demolished
(555 Sylvan Drive)
Winter Park, 1934, 1938

Wallis R. Kinney
Kinney and Richards Apartments
Multifamily units
Winter Park, 1952

L. J. Lazerlere
Residence
Interlachen Avenue
Winter Park, 1948

Tracy Lay
Alterations to residence
617 Interlachen Avenue
Winter Park, 1939
(formerly Noyes house)

Tracy Lay
Residence
111 North Ivanhoe Boulevard
Orlando, 1948

Thomas G. Lee
Residence
317 North Bumby Avenue
Orlando, 1962

William B. Leggett
Residence—demolished
Winter Park, 1949

James F. Lehan
Residence
292 Sylvan Boulevard—altered
Winter Park, 1951

Edgar C. Leonard
Residence—extensively
  remodeled in 1990s
915 Old England Avenue
Winter Park, 1937

W. B. Louthan
Dining room
Mount Dora, 1948

Colonel Edward Lowry
Residence
301 Sylvan Drive
Winter Park, 1941

Archibald F. McAllaster
Residence
160 Alexander Place
Winter Park, 1934

Duncan T. McEwan
Residence
407 Peachtree
Orlando, 1938

Ray McCaffrey
Residence
Clermont, 1951

Arthur McGugan
Alterations to apartments
846 North Park Avenue
Winter Park, 1948

Arthur McGugan
Residence
669 Osceola Avenue
Winter Park, 1948

Arthur McGugan
Alterations to residence
Winter Park, n.d.

Scott C. McGuire
Residence
1215 Via Salerno
Winter Park, 1952

Hugh McKean
Residence
Bonita Drive
Winter Park, 1952, 1961

Hugh McKean
Residence
231 North Interlachen Avenue
Winter Park, 1946

John R. McPherson
Residence
711 Alba Drive
Orlando, 1950

R. F. Maguire
Residence
Windermere, 1951

Alvin A. Marriott
Alterations to residence—
  demolished
(1227 Gene Street)
Winter Park, 1947

George S. Marsh
Residence
1020 Palmer Avenue
Winter Park, 1954
(formerly Plant house)

Rudy D. Matthews
Residence
235 Fawsett Road
Winter Park, 1949

L. W. Menard
Residence
Daytona, 1965

Harry G. Miller
Residence
2174 Glencoe Road
Winter Park, 1950
(later Thomas Pinel)

William C. Mitchell
Alterations to residence
1430 Elizabeth Drive
Winter Park, 1970
(formerly George C. Holt house)

Mildred Mizener
Residence
225 Palmer Avenue
Winter Park, 1939

R. W. Moorhead
Residence
[no address, n.d.]

Woodbury T. Morris
Alterations and remodeling
916 Palmer Avenue
Winter Park, 1937
Guest cottage, 1946

Robert C. Mumby
Residence
4620 Wayfarer Place
Orlando, 1971

Mildred Mizener Residence

Woodbury T. Morris Alterations and remodeling

Mrs. Peyton Musselwhite
Alteration to garage apartment
668 Osceola Avenue
Winter Park, 1939

W. W. Nelson
Residence
802 Georgia Avenue
Winter Park, 1952

E. M. Newald
Residence
1300 Country Club Drive
Orlando, 1937

James B. Newman
Cottage
Lake Fairview
Winter Park, 1951

J. W. Newton
Residence
[1141 Morse Boulevard?]
Winter Park, 1934

M. B. Newton
Alterations to cottage
[1668 Lasbury Avenue?]
Winter Park, 1941

F. W. Nickel
Residence
[1250 College Point?]
Winter Park, 1955

George L. Noyes
Residence
617 Interlachen Avenue
Winter Park, 1934

H. N. Oakley
Residence
1952

Rockwell C. Osborne
Residence
852 Georgia Avenue
Winter Park, 1939

Gilbert S. Osincup
Residence
3316 Lake Shore Drive
Orlando, 1938

Mrs. E. W. Packard
Alterations to residence
[2506 Elizabeth Drive?]
Winter Park, [1933?]

Harold Pate
Residence
2175 Via Tuscany
Winter Park, 1975

Terry B. Patterson
Alterations and additions
  to residence
1023 Lakeview Drive—altered
Winter Park, 1949

Admiral B. F. Perry
Residence
Clermont, 1951

Thomas H. Pinel
Alterations and additions
  to residence
2174 Glencoe
Winter Park, 1970

Mrs. C. Griggs Plant
Residence
1020 Palmer Avenue
Winter Park, 1939

H. T. Price
Residence
Lake Placid, 1947

Morgan W. Price Jr.
Studies for residence
[530 West Park Avenue?]
Winter Park, 1941

Eve Proctor
Studies for residence
[340 Cherokee Lane?]
Winter Park, 1953

Helen Purdue
Storage building
[328 North Park Avenue #3, 5?]
Winter Park, 1946

Carl R. Ragnitt
Residence
1080 North Park Avenue
Winter Park, 1951

George D. Randall
Residence and cottage
Sarasota, n.d.

J. W. Rankin
Residence
1330 Lake Knowles Circle
Winter Park, 1940

Wilson Reed
Residence
1202 Lancaster Drive
Orlando, 1949

Mrs. F. J. Reilly
Addition
1660 Lasbury Avenue
Winter Park, 1951

John H. Rhodes
Residence
1400 Green Cove Road
Winter Park, 1950

Newton Rich
Studies for residence
400 Lakewood Drive
[Trismen Terrace?]
Winter Park, 1955

William C. Richards
Apartments
Interlachen Avenue
Winter Park, 1952

Robert Richardson
Studies for residence
Clarcona, n.d.

Roberts
Studies for residence
St. Petersburg, n.d.

John D. Rockefeller Jr.
Alterations to residence
The Casements
Ormond Beach, 1938

James Gamble Rogers
Residence—demolished
(3 Isle of Sicily)
Four Winds
Winter Park, 1929
Alterations to cottage, 1937

Gamble Rogers Apartments
Unbuilt
Multifamily units
Winter Park, 1940

James Gamble Rogers
Guest cottage
3 Isle of Sicily
Winter Park, 1946

James Gamble Rogers
Unbuilt residence
1290 Palmer Avenue
Winter Park, 1946

James Gamble Rogers
Residence
Temple Grove
1290 Palmer Avenue
(now 1011 Temple Grove Drive)
Winter Park, 1948

Mrs. John A. Rogers
Residence
DeLand, 1948

Howard L. Roney
Addition to portico
[1399 Indiana Avenue?]
Winter Park, 1941

Henry C. Rowe
Residence
Daytona Beach, 1931

John R. Royer
Residence
704 Kiwi Court
Winter Park, 1984

Fletcher Rush
Residence
508 Lakeview Avenue
Orlando, 1955

James Gamble Rogers,
Temple Grove Residence

*Mrs. William C. Sanders
Residence*

Frank Russell
Residence
Fern Park, 1939

Mrs. William C. Sanders
Residence
921 Georgia Avenue
Winter Park, 1935

J. Hilbert Sapp
Alterations and additions
  to residence
801 Seville at Alameda
Orlando, 1952

Charles F. Schmidt
Residence
312 Palmer Avenue
Winter Park, 1935

William A. Scott
Residence
540 Interlachen Avenue
Winter Park, 1933

Bertram D. Scott
Residence
825 Bonita Drive
Winter Park, 1941

*Charles F. Schmidt
Residence*

Thomas A. Scott Jr.
Alterations to residence
240 King's Way
Winter Park, 1946

Edgar V. Seeler
Residence
730 Via Lugano—altered
Winter Park, 1949

Arthur B. Seibold
Residence
1090 Eben Holden Drive
(now 39 Palmer Avenue)
Winter Park, 1941

Harry L. Shearer
Residence
350 Killarney Drive
Winter Park, 1952

Marion Shepard
Alterations to garage
Winter Park, 1942

Eugene R. Shippen
Residence for Eugene L. Jewett
Tree Tops
1280 North Park Avenue
Winter Park, 1937

Eugene R. Shippen
Residence
1290 North Park Avenue
Winter Park, 1931

Arthur Schultz
Alterations and additions
   to residence
Maitland, 1949

W. M. Slemmons III
Residence
530 Lakeview
Orlando, 1976

Mrs. Rock Sleyster
Residence
311 North Interlachen Avenue
Winter Park, 1952

Charles Smith
Residence
Pensacola, 1946
Addition to porch, 1953

F. Burton Smith
Residence
400 Lakeview
Orlando, 1950

Everett C. Somers
Residence

Harry Smith
Residence
Winter Garden, n.d.

Helena K. Smith
Ferneries
Fern Park, ca. 1930

J. E. Smith
Studies for residence
Leesburg, 1946

Percy Ford Smith
Residence
Winter Park, 1952

Rhea Smith
Residence—demolished
(600 Bonita Drive)
Winter Park, 1939

Mrs. Shelby Smith
Addition to residence
875 Old England Avenue
Winter Park, n.d.

Shelby Smith Jr.
Residence
Pensacola, 1940

Everett C. Somers
Residence
1475 Gore Terrace
Winter Park, 1949

Mrs. Henry G. Sommer
Residence
Peoria, Ill., 1953

Richard Spencer
Residence
Dundee, 1949

Alexander Sprunt Jr.
Residence
Charleston, S.C., 1932
(in association with David B. Hyer)

Edwin M. Stanton
Residence
350 Henckel Circle
Winter Park, 1939

Harold Stein
Residence
833 Seville Place
Orlando, 1938

Jessie M. Stevens
Residence
Ormond Beach, n.d.

Harold Stein Residence

R. E. Stevens
Studies for residences
Allendale, n.d.

Ted Strawn
Residence
DeLand, 1942

Hope Strong
Garage
[149 Chelton Circle?]
Winter Park, 1947

Walter H. Tappan
Residence
490 Webster
Winter Park, ca. 1930

John G. Tapper
Residence
222 Alexander Place
Winter Park, 1940

James J. Taylor
Alterations to residence
Ocala, 1937

J. Clagett Taylore
Residence
Sebring, 1949

George Temple
Cottage
Daytona, n.d.

Walter H. Tappan Residence

*A. T. Traylor
Residence*

George Temple Jr.
Residence
[701 E. Concord?]
Orlando, [1939?]

Alvin D. Thayer
Residence
2010 Fawsett Road
Winter Park, 1939

James B. Thomas
Alterations to residence
1561 Via Tuscany
Winter Park, n.d.

R. M. Thompson
Cottage
Erie, Pa., 1931

John Tiedtke
Additions
2 Isle of Sicily
Winter Park, 1952, 1963, 1988
(formerly Burress house)

Colonel Cyril C. Train
Residence
1534 Lakeshore Drive
Orlando, 1960

A. T. Traylor
Residence
Fern Park, ca. 1928

F. D. Trismen
Addition to residence; outbuildings
707 Osceola Drive
Winter Park, 1937

Richard F. Trismen
Residence
Winter Park, 1971

Alexander Buel Trowbridge
Residence
320 Sylvan Boulevard
Winter Park, 1939

F. R. Trunells
Tourist cottages
Casselberry, 1939

J. W. Tucker Jr.
Residence
740 Palmer Avenue
Winter Park, 1954

W. Turner
Cottage
Fern Park, 1931

George C. Tuttle
Residence
Maitland, 1937

Harold Van Buren
Residence
200 Chase Avenue
Winter Park, 1941

J.W.W. Walker
Residence
279 Virginia Drive
Winter Park, 1947

George Warner
Alterations to residence
[337 Interlachen Avenue?]
[486 Virginia Court Avenue?]
Winter Park, 1926

Mrs. Samuel A. Weissenberger
Alterations and additions
   to residence
789 Bonita Drive
Winter Park, 1947

J. M. Wells
Screened porch
Winter Park, n.d.

James Wesley
Alterations and additions
   to residence
1601 Oakhurst
Winter Park, 1952

Otto Wettstein
Residence
Ocala, 1948

Carl Weyland
Garage apartment
115 Palmer Avenue
Winter Park, 1949

Henry A. White
Residence
Webster and Golfview
Winter Park, 1964

*Alexander Buel Trowbridge
Residence*

C. Arthur Yergey
Residence

Nancy B. White
Residence
641 Knowles Avenue
Winter Park, 1933

F.E.L. Whitesel
Studies for residence
1953

E. Reed Whittle
Residence
279 Virginia Drive
Winter Park, 1947

R. H. Williams
Residence
Eustis, 1941

Albert Frederick Wilson
La Tourette
Residence
128 S. Halifax Avenue
Ormond Beach, 1937

Joseph C. Wilson
Residence
145 Palmer Avenue
Winter Park, 1951

Colonel Osborn C. Wilson
Residence
646 Seminole Drive
Winter Park, 1948

W. H. Winslow
Residence
1244 Mayfiled
Winter Park, 1941
Alterations, 1953

I. A. Wones
Bungalow
Lake Butler, n.d.

Ernest Wright
Residence
Gainesville, 1961

James Wright
Residence
Winter Park, 1927

Tom Yandre
Residence
Orlando, 1948

C. Arthur Yergey
Residence
505 Peachtree
(now 735 Edgewater)
Orlando, 1934

G. T. Zittroue
Residence
Orlando, n.d.

Notes

Chapter 1. The Rogers Family

1. Keith McKean, interview with James Gamble Rogers II, 1; Aaron Betsky, *James Gamble Rogers*, 9, states that Joseph Martin Rogers sold insurance, and his eldest son, Bernard Fowler Rogers (b. 1864), followed his father into that profession. The source for this information is a notation in James Gamble Rogers I's Yale Class Book for 1889, in which Rogers stated that his father "is in the insurance business." Rogers family scrapbooks indicate that Joseph Martin Rogers attended Union College in Schenectedy, New York, then graduated from the Louisville University (sic) Law School and later the Albany Law School, known as the nation's oldest independent private law school. The scrapbook also states that Joseph Martin Rogers practiced law in Columbus, Indiana, for several years, until he went into the fire insurance business. In 1881 he was made manager of the Western Department (in Chicago) of the Queen Insurance Company of Liverpool, England.

2. McKean, 1.

3. Marjorie Muller, interview with James Gamble Rogers II, 1.

4. Betsky, 9. The family's move would have been while Joseph Martin Rogers was married to his first wife, Katherine Mary Gamble (1844–1889), with whom he had seven children. In 1892, a few years after Katherine's death, Rogers married his second wife, Julia Rogers (1850–1924), without issue. The Rogers family did not move to Chicago before 1870, however, since it is known that John Arthur Rogers (the younger brother to James Gamble Rogers I) was born in Louisville. The Rogers family scrapbook contains a large collection of genealogy that traces the family roots back to Thomas Rogers, who arrived in Plymouth on the ship *Mayflower* in 1620 with Governor Bradford. See also Alice Wilma Andrews Westgate, *Mayflower Families through Five Generations*, 153–55ff. Elizabeth Hart Baird, James Gamble Rogers II's mother, also traced her family back to a *Mayflower* passenger, Thomas Beard (later changed to Baird). Beard, a Scot, was born in 1608 and came to New England in 1629 aboard the *Mayflower* with Governor Endicott. Beard was a cobbler. Elizabeth recounts her family's genealogy in the book she wrote and published privately about her mother, Elizabeth Mather Warner Baird (1837–1928), *Glimpses into a Glorious Life*.

5. Betsky, 10–11.

6. Betsky, 11. Yale did not offer a degree program in architecture until 1905; Rogers most likely graduated with a general arts degree.

7. Jenney graduated from the École Centrale des Arts et Manufactures in Paris in 1856 and entered the Union Army in 1861, in which he served as chief engineer of the Fifteenth Army Corps, Army of Tennessee. Discharged in 1866, with the rank of major, Jenney came to Chicago in 1867 and established his office the next year. While many have argued whether Jenney was more an engineer than architect (Louis Sullivan thought of him as the former), his work gives evidence that he was both. For more, see Carl W. Condit, *The Chicago School of Architecture*, 28ff.

8. Betsky, 11.

9. Betsky, 16.

10. For additional information on the philosophy and teachings of the École des Beaux-Arts during this period, see Arthur Drexler, ed., *The Architecture of the École des Beaux-Arts*.

11. Henry F. Withey and Elsie Rathburn Withey, *Biographical Dictionary of American Architects (Deceased)*, 522.

12. Betsky, 18–19; Withey and Withey, 523.

13. Betsky, 22.

14. Robert C. Twombly, *Frank Lloyd Wright*, 35.

15. Betsky, 31; Withey and Withey, 522–23.

16. Betsky, 79–80.

17. For more on the Yale commissions and Rogers' relationship with the Harknesses, see Betsky, 33ff., and Patrick L. Pinnell, *The Campus Guide: Yale University*.

18. Betsky, 261–67.

19. The gates were executed by Polish-born craftsman and metalsmith Sam Yellin (1885–1940) of Philadelphia. Yellin also completed the gates for Rogers' Hall of Graduate Studies (1932). Pinnell, 62, 100.

20. Betsky, 258, n. 1.

21. Withey and Withey, 522.

22. Kevin B. Leonard, University Archives, Northwestern University Library, personal communication with Debra A. McClane, February 24, 2003.

23. Information provided to authors by Registrar's Office, MIT, February 20, 2003.

24. Adolf K. Placzek, *Macmillan Encyclopedia of Architects*, 59.

25. Betsky, 243, n. 31; Withey and Withey, 523.

26. McKean, 2.

27. The slogan has since been modified to "the world's most famous beach."

28. McKean, 3; Muller, 2; Naval Historical Center, Online Library of Selected Images, Civilian Ships, http://www.history.navy.mil/photos/sh-civil/civsh-d.htm (accessed April 4, 2003).

29. Pleasant Daniel Gold, *History of Volusia County, Florida*, 277.

30. Gold, 277; James Gamble Rogers II, letter to Mrs. John E. Hebel, Volusia County Historical Commission, February 14, 1967.

31. Betsky, 35.

32. "Golden Anniversary for Art League," *Daytona Beach News-Journal*, ca. 1982, clipping in vertical files of Halifax Historical Society, Daytona, Beach, Florida.

33. Daytona Beach High School, *The Sentinel*, 34.

34. McKean, 3.

35. National Civilian Personnel Center, James Gamble Rogers II, application form 8.

36. John Hopewell Rogers, interview with the authors, Winter Park, Florida, March 2003.

37. Dartmouth College Library, Alumni Records, James Gamble Rogers II.

38. McKean, 4; Muller, 4.

39. John Hopewell Rogers, interview with the authors, Winter Park, Florida, September 1993; John Hopewell Rogers, nomination application for James Gamble Rogers II as Fellow in the American Institute of Architects.

Chapter 2. Beginning in Winter Park

1. National Bank of Commerce, *Millennium Memories*, 3–4. In 1858 David Mizell Jr. had purchased a small plot of land in the area, calling it "Lake View." But it was Loring Chase's vision that eventually created the town. Lake View was renamed "Osceola" in 1870 and later incorporated into Chase's Winter Park. Mark Derr, *Some Kind of Paradise*, 81.

2. National Bank of Commerce, 7.

3. Derr, 81.

4. McKean, 7. Gamble Rogers cited Windsong in Winter Park, home of Hugh McKean and Jeanette Genius McKean, built in 1938, and The Ripples in Orlando as good examples of Spanish architecture in the area. He also recalled that both houses were designed by an architect named Krug.

5. "The House of James Gamble Rogers II," *House Beautiful*, January 1932, 814–16.

6. *Fern Park Estates*, real estate brochure, ca. 1926. Courtesy of Hibbard Casselberry Jr.

7. James Gamble Rogers II, "Barbour House," unpublished manuscript, n.d. Copy on file at Rogers, Lovelock, and Fritz, Inc.

8. *60 Years of Architecture by James Gamble Rogers II*, exhibit pamphlet commemorating opening of the Olin Library, Cornell Fine Arts Center, Rollins College, Winter Park, Florida, 3.

9. McKean, 10, 11.

10. McKean, 4, 5.

11. *Florida Architecture and Allied Arts*, published by Florida AIA chapters from 1935 to 1942 and followed by *Florida Architecture*, printed "the work of members and associates who from the point of view of the profession

are practicing in accordance with the standard of the Institute." Richard Kiehnel was the publisher and sat on the editorial board until his death in 1942. The magazine was published in Miami from the Seybold building, where Kiehnel had his offices. *Architecturally Winter Park* and *Orlando and Winter Park Architecturally* were printed throughout the 1930s by the Sixth District of the Florida Association of Architects. Rogers' work frequently appeared in all of these publications.

12. "Rogers' 'Jolly Roger' Wins First Place," *Winter Park Topics*, February 22, 1934, 1.

13. "Architects Discuss Community Beauty," *Winter Park Topics*, February 8, 1936, 1, 4. For more information on early efforts to beautify the American city, see William H. Wilson, *The City Beautiful Movement*.

14. James Gamble Rogers II, "Termite Control," *Architectural Forum*, December 1935, 542. The article was subsequently reprinted by the *New York Sun* newspaper (1936) and *Better Homes and Gardens* magazine (Summer 1938).

15. "A Historic Cottage," *Orlando Sentinel*, September 12, 1992, sec. G.

16. McKean, 16.

17. Ronald B. Hartzer, *To Great and Useful Purpose*, 72.

18. Lt. Col. J. T. Knight Jr., letter to Mr. J. G. Rogers II, February 26, 1944.

19. Hartzer, 71.

20. Knight, letter to Rogers.

21. John Hopewell Rogers, nomination application for James Gamble Rogers II as Fellow in the American Institute of Architects.

22. Muller, 22.

23. Muller, 23.

24. James Gamble Rogers II, "Modern Jail for Small County," *American City*, August 1957, 137.

25. [Florida A&M Hospital], *Hospital Management*, May 1951.

26. "Test of Time Award," *Florida Architect*, November/December 1992, 21. Rogers participated on the team that developed the 1947 Capitol Center Plan. The project was under the direction of Herbert L. Flint, with Albert Davis Taylor, a noted Cleveland landscape architect, as consultant.

27. "Restoration Group Suggests Another Survey of Cordova," [*St. Augustine Record*], December 12, 1961.

28. Ed Hayes, "The Magical Pencil of James Gamble Rogers," *Orlando Sentinel*, September 2, 1979, Florida Magazine, 13.

29. Hayes, 7; Suzanne Hupp, "Timeless Treasures," *Orlando Sentinel*, February 24, 1990.

30. Hayes, 13.

Chapter 3. Developing an Architectural Character

1. "An Ideal for the Small Southern Town," [*American Home*] [ca. 1931]. Copy on file at Rogers, Lovelock, and Fritz, Inc.

2. McKean, 11.

3. "Colonial Clicks Wherever It Goes," *Better Homes and Gardens*, April 1940, 78.

4. "Colonial Clicks Wherever It Goes," 78.

5. "House of James Gamble Rogers II," *Architectural Forum*, October 1935, 352.

6. John Hopewell Rogers, interview with authors, Winter Park, Florida, September 1993.

Chapter 4. The Legacy

1. Pecky cypress is a type of cypress wood that is characterized by dark markings and distinctive patterning caused by a natural fungus that is killed once the tree is harvested. While Florida Cracker houses often used the wood, it was considered nearly worthless to the building trade because of its "imperfections." This view changed in the 1920s, when Addison Mizner, who claimed credit for "discovering" the wood, began using it in many of his Palm Beach houses. Rogers used pecky cypress for paneling, woodwork, and ceilings. Coquina rock is a naturally occurring sedimentary stone created by broken shell and quartz and is found along the eastern coast of Florida. The rock is relatively soft and easy to cut, but hardens upon exposure to air. Spaniards used the stone to construct the Castillo de San Marcos and many other buildings in St. Augustine. The stone is often finished with whitewash or plaster.

2. Newcomb, 30.

3. [Rogers] "An Ideal for the Small Southern Town."

4. McKean, 12–13.

5. Ibid., 14.

Chapter 5. Selected Houses

1. James Gamble Rogers II, "The Rogers House on the Isle of Sicily," unpublished manuscript, n.d. Copy on file at Rogers, Lovelock, and Fritz, Inc.

2. John Hopewell Rogers, interview with the authors, March 2003.

3. "House of James Gamble Rogers II," *Architectural Forum*, 352.

4. "Dr. Eugene R. Shippen, Distinguished Minister, Observing 90th Birthday," *Winter Park Topics*, January 28, 1955, 1.

5. Walter Muir Whitehall, *Dumbarton Oaks*, 55.

6. Whitehall, 56.

7. Whitehall, 56.

8. Whitehall, 56.

9. "Dr. Eugene R. Shippen," *Winter Park Topics*, January 28, 1955, 11.

10. "Dr. Eugene R. Shippen," *Winter Park Topics*, January 28, 1955, 11.

11. Some of the more notable events that occurred at the house include Dr. Shippen's ninetieth and ninety-second birthdays, the marriage of the Shippens' granddaughter Elizabeth Blount Shippen to George Whitfield Mercer, and the marriage of daughter Zoe Shippen to Laurent Varnum.

12. "Local Couple Furnish Unitarian Altar," *Winter Park Sun*, December 2, 1954.

13. "Dr. Eugene R. Shippen," *Winter Park Topics*, January 28, 1955, 11.

14. "Mr. Barbour Dies in Winter Park," *Orlando Morning Sentinel*, April 12, 1950.

15. Rogers, "Barbour House."

16. *Winter Park Herald*, February 9, 1933.

17. "Spanish Evening at Barbour Residence," *Winter Park Topics*, April 9, 1938, 1; "Spanish Fiesta in Cervantes [sic] Honor," *Winter Park Topics*, April 15, 1939.

18. Newcomb, 25.

19. Newcomb, 79.

20. State of Florida Division of Historical Resources, Florida master site file, "Barbour House."

21. "The Barbour House," *Winter Park Topics*, February 15, 1936.

22. Penney Retirement Community, *Life More Abundant*, 1–21 passim.

23. Rogers, "Barbour House."

24. "The Barbour House," *Winter Park Topics*, February 15, 1936.

25. Having produced many of the best-known statues of Abraham Lincoln in the country, Ganiere (1866–1935) became known as "the Lincoln sculptor" in the early twentieth century. In 1932 he produced four sculptures for the Florida exhibit at the Century of Progress International Exposition held in Chicago. Among these sculptures was *The Spirit of Florida*, a 7'9" figure of a woman with her arms raised holding a giant orange, and a 6'3" statue of Ponce de Leon.

26. *Winter Park Herald*, February 9, 1933.

27. "The Barbour House," *Winter Park Topics*, February 15, 1936.

28. Sandra Mathers, "Winter Park Stops Wrecking Ball at Casa Feliz," *Orlando Sentinel Reporter-Star*, September 13, 2000, sec. A.

29. "New Barbour Apartments," advertisement in *Winter Park Topics*, January 14, 1939.

30. "New Barbour Apartments Augment Architectural Beauty of Winter Park," *Winter Park Topics*, January 21, 1939, 6.

31. McKean, 14.

32. *Winter Park Topics*, January 21, 1939, 6.

33. Nancy A. Jarzombek, *The Glow of Sunlight*, 2–4.

34. Jarzombek, 4–5; Mantle Fielding, *Dictionary of American Painters, Sculptors and Engravers*, 673.

35. Jarzombek, 7.

36. "The Barbour House," *Winter Park Topics*, February 15, 1936.

37. Rollins College Archives, George C. Holt biographical information.

38. Nina Oliver Dean, "A Knight and a Maiden Fair," *Orlando Sentinel*, May 24, 1936.

39. "'Tree Tops,' New Home of Dr. and Mrs. Jewett," *Winter Park Topics,* February 26, 1938, 7.

40. "'Tree Tops,' New Home of Dr. and Mrs. Jewett," *Winter Park Topics,* February 26, 1938, 7.

41. "For Rent for Next Season, $900," advertisement, *Winter Park Topics,* March 28, 1941.

42. "Edgar C. Leonard," *Winter Park Topics,* March 19, 1938, 4.

43. McKean, 8.

44. Edward Durell Stone, *Evolution of an Architect,* 32–33.

45. *Winter Park Topics,* April 15, 1939, 8.

46. "Mrs. Plant's Will Aids Genteel Poor," *Orlando Sentinel Reporter-Star,* [ca. June 1947].

47. "Rollins Gets $10,000 from Plant Estate," [*Orlando Sentinel Reporter-Star*], June 13, 1947.

48. For an excellent discussion of the myriad forms and expressions of the Colonial Revival style, see the essays in Alan Axelrod, *The Colonial Revival in America.*

49. James Gamble Rogers II, "Mizener House," unpublished manuscript, n.d. Copy on file at Rogers, Lovelock, and Fritz, Inc.

50. Suzanne Hupp, "An Architect's Contribution: How James Gamble Rogers Defined the Charm of a Community," *Orlando Sentinel,* June 20, 1987, sec. G.

Bibliography

Axelrod, Alan, ed. *The Colonial Revival in America.* New York: Norton, 1985.

Betsky, Aaron. *James Gamble Rogers and the Architecture of Pragmatism.* New York: Architectural History Foundation; Cambridge, Mass.: MIT Press, 1994.

Campen, Richard N. *Winter Park Portrait: The Story of Winter Park and Rollins College.* Beachwood, Ohio: West Summit Press, [1987].

Chapman, Robin. *The Absolutely Essential Guide to Winter Park: The Village in the Heart of Central Florida.* Privately published, 2001.

"Colonial Clicks Wherever It Goes." *Better Homes and Gardens*, April 1940, 78–79.

Condit, Carl W. *The Chicago School of Architecture.* Chicago: University of Chicago Press, 1964.

Curl, Donald W. *Mizner's Florida: American Resort Architecture.* New York: Architectural History Foundation; Cambridge, Mass.: MIT Press, 1984.

Daytona Beach High School, Volusia County Public Schools, *The Sentinel*, 1918. Copy in the collection of the Halifax Historical Society, Daytona Beach, Fla.

Derr, Mark. *Some Kind of Paradise: A Chronicle of Man and the Land in Florida.* New York: William Morrow, 1989.

Drexler, Arthur, ed. *The Architecture of the École des Beaux-Arts.* New York: Museum of Modern Art; Cambridge, Mass.: MIT Press, ca. 1977.

Fern Park Estates. Real estate brochure, ca. 1926. Courtesy of Hibbard Casselberry Jr.

Fielding, Mantle. *Dictionary of American Painters, Sculptors and Engravers.* 2nd ed., ed. Glenn B. Opitz. Poughkeepsie, N.Y.; Apollo, ca. 1986.

[Florida A&M Hospital]. *Hospital Management*, May 1951.

Gold, Pleasant Daniel. *History of Volusia County, Florida.* DeLand, Fla.: E.O. Painter Printing Company, 1927.

Hartzer, Ronald B. *To Great and Useful Purpose: A History of the Wilmington District U.S. Army Corps of Engineers.* [Wilmington, N.C.]: The Corps, ca. 1984.

Hayes, Ed. "The Magical Pencil of James Gamble Rogers." *Orlando Sentinel*, September 2, 1979, Florida Magazine, 7–10, 13.

"House of James Gamble Rogers II." *Architectural Forum*, October 1935, 352–53.

"The House of James Gamble Rogers II." *House Beautiful*, January 1932, 814–16.

Jarzombek, Nancy A. *The Glow of Sunlight: Paintings by George L. Noyes (1864–1954), October 13 to November 28, 1998.* Boston: Vose Galleries, ca. 1998.

Knight, Lt. Col. J. T., Jr. Letter to James Gamble Rogers II, February 26, 1944. Copy held within the National Civilian Personnel Records for James Gamble Rogers II. National Archives and Records Administration, St. Louis, Mo.

McKean, Keith. Interview with James Gamble Rogers II, October 27, 1981. Transcript, Winter Park Public Library, Winter Park, Fla.

Muller, Marjorie R. Interview for the Morse Foundation with Mr. James Gamble Rogers II, November 14, 1981. Transcript, Winter Park Public Library, Winter Park, Fla.

National Bank of Commerce. *Millennium Memories.* [Winter Park, Fla.]: National Bank of Commerce, 1999.

National Civilian Personnel Records. Records for James Gamble Rogers II. National Archives and Records Administration, St. Louis, Mo.

Newcomb, Rexford. *The Spanish House for America: Its Design, Furnishing, and Garden.* Philadelphia: Lippincott, 1927.

Penney Retirement Community. *Life More Abundant: The Story of a Retirement Community at Penney Farms, Florida.* Penney Farms, Fla.: Privately published, 1973.

Pinnell, Patrick L. *The Campus Guide: Yale University.* New York: Princeton Architectural Press, 1999.

Placzek, Adolf K. *Macmillan Encyclopedia of Architects.* New York: Free Press, 1982.

Rogers, Elizabeth Hart Baird. *Glimpses into a Glorious Life.* Daytona Beach, Fla.: Privately published, 1932.

Rogers Family Scrapbooks. Courtesy of John Hopewell Rogers, Winter Park, Fla.

[Rogers, James Gamble II] "An Ideal for the Small Southern Town." No publication information available. *American Home*, ca. 1931.

Rogers, James Gamble II. "Barbour House." Unpublished manuscript, n.d. Courtesy of Rogers, Lovelock, and Fritz, Inc., Winter Park, Fla.

———. "Mizener House." Unpublished manuscript, n.d. Copy on file at Rogers, Lovelock, and Fritz, Inc., Winter Park, Fla.

———. "Modern Jail for Small County." *American City*, August 1957, 137.

———. "The Rogers House on the Isle of Sicily." Unpublished manuscript, n.d. Courtesy of Rogers, Lovelock, and Fritz, Inc., Winter Park, Fla.

———. "Termite Control." *Architectural Forum*, December 1935, 542–43.

Rogers, John Hopewell. Interviews with the authors, Winter Park, Fla., September 1993, March 2003.

Rogers, John Hopewell [sponsor]. Nomination application for James Gamble

Rogers II as Fellow in the American Institute of Architects, 1990. Courtesy of Rogers, Lovelock, and Fritz, Inc., Winter Park, Fla.

Rollins College Archives. Biographical Information on George C. Holt. Winter Park, Fla.: Olin Library, ca. 1993.

60 Years of Architecture by James Gamble Rogers II. Exhibit pamphlet. [Winter Park, Fla.]: Rollins College, 1985.

Stone, Edward Durell. *Evolution of an Architect.* New York: Horizon, 1962.

"Test of Time Award." *Florida Architect,* November/December 1992, 21.

Twombly, Robert C. *Frank Lloyd Wright: His Life and His Architecture.* New York: John Wiley, 1979.

Westgate, Alice Wilma Andrews, compiler. *Mayflower Families through Five Generations.* Vol. 2, *Chilton More Rogers.* Plymouth, Mass.: General Society of *Mayflower* Descendents, 1978.

Whitehall, Walter Muir. *Dumbarton Oaks: The History of a Georgetown House and Garden, 1800–1966.* Cambridge, Mass.: Belknap Press of Harvard University Press, 1967.

Wilson, William H. *The City Beautiful Movement.* Baltimore: Johns Hopkins University Press, ca. 1989.

Withey, Henry F., and Elsie Rathburn Withey. *Biographical Dictionary of American Architects (Deceased).* Los Angeles: New Age, 1956.

Index

Absolutely Essential Guide to Winter Park, The (Chapman), xv
Adair, Lake: Keene house on, 130
AIA (American Institute of Architects), Florida chapters: State Craftsmanship Award, 32; Test of Time Award, 40; Medal of Honor, 43; Rogers' involvement in, xviii, 28; Mid-Florida chapter of, xviii, 28; publications of, 155–56n11
Alberta Drive, 104
Alexander Place, 91–92
American Home (magazine): publication of Rogers' Traylor and Smith houses, 24, 25; Harold Haliday Costain, photographer for, 26
Architectural Forum (magazine): publishes Rogers' article "Termite Control" (1935), 28–29; *The 1936 Book of Small Homes*, 46, 62; as design source, 52, 125
Architectural revivalism. *See* Revivalism, architectural
Architecturally Winter Park (magazine), 27
Armstrong, Frank (contractor), 75
Art Moderne (style), elements of, 107. *See also* Jewett house [Tree Tops]
Aux Tours D'Argent (Noyes design shop), 89
Awards (received by Rogers): State Craftsmanship (AIA), Olin Library, 32; Outstanding Service, U.S. Military (Korean War), 34–35; Best Small Jail of the Year (1956), 36; Hamilton Holt, Rollins College (1984), 41–42; honorary degree, University of Central Florida (1976), 42; Outstanding Citizen, Winter Park (1986), 42; honorary degree, Rollins College (1986), 42; Certificate of Recognition, Mid-Florida chapter, AIA (1985), 42–43; Medal of Honor, Mid-Florida chapter, AIA (1990), 43; Fellowship, American Institute of Architects (AIA) (1991), 43; Test of Time, Florida Supreme Court Building (1992), 40

Barbour, Nettie (patron), 70. *See also* Barbour house
Barbour, Robert Bruce (patron); admires Rogers' Four Winds, 25–26, 53–54, 62; biography, 69, 82–83. *See also* Barbour Apartments; Barbour house
Barbour Apartments, 82–84. *See also* Barbour, Robert Bruce
Barbour house [Casa Feliz]: illustrations, ii, 71, 73, 74, 75, 76, 77, 78, 79, 81; general, 54, 69–82; description, 70–79; interior design, 80, 81; social events at, 70. *See also* Barbour, Robert Bruce; Noyes, Mabel
Bear Island. *See* Isle of Sicily
Betsky, Aaron (author), *James Gamble Rogers I and the Architecture of Pragmatism*, xix, 2
Better Homes and Gardens (magazine), 46, 125
Bingham, Doris (patron), 27
Bledsoe, L. V., house, 46–47, 47
Bonita Drive, 20
Boosterism, 9, 17–18, 44. *See also* Florida real estate boom; Tourism, Florida
Borden, Gail and Elsa, 116–17. *See also* Leonard house

Bradley, U. T. [Udolpho Theodore] (patron), 27, 32
Brewer, Edward Hill, 20
Brown, Ervin Theodore (patron), 32
Building materials. *See* Regionalism, architectural
Burnham, Daniel H. (architect), 2
Burnham and Root (architecture firm), 2–3
Burress, Paul (patron), 117. *See also* Burress house
Burress house [Tiedtke house]: illustrations, *119, 120 (plan), color plates 8, 9, 10;* siting of, 117; description of, 118–20; alterations and additions to, 119–20. *See also* Isle of Sicily; Revivalism, architectural; Tudor Revival (style)
Butler, Jonathan (architect), 7
Butler Rogers Baskett Architects (firm), 7

Campen, Richard N. (author), *Winter Park Portrait,* xv
Camp, Victor N., 21. *See also* Camp house
Camp house (Ormond Beach): illustration, *22;* description of, 21–23, 59–60
Capitol Center Plan (Tallahassee), 38–40, 156n26
Carrère and Hastings (architects), xvii
Casa Feliz. *See* Barbour house
Casa Feliz, Friends of, 82
Casselberry, Florida: Rogers' work in, 21
Casselberry, Hibbard, Sr. (patron): developer of Fern Park, 23, 25, 26; caught in hurricane with Rogers, 29–30
Chabot, Earl (contractor), 111
Chapman, Oliver E. (real estate developer), 17–18. *See also* Winter Park, development of
Chapman, Robin (author), *The Absolutely Essential Guide to Winter Park,* xv
Chase, Loring P. (real estate developer), 17–18. *See also* Winter Park, development of
Chase, Warren L. (architect), 41

Chicago, Illinois: Rogers family connection with, 1–5, 7–8, 11; Winter Park connection with, 15, 17, 20
Chicago Architectural Club, 4
Chicago School (of architecture), 2–3
Clark, Herbert L. (specifications writer), 41
Classical Revival (style): Beaux-Arts, xvii; of Winter Park Women's Club, 21. *See also* Florida Supreme Court Building; Revivalism, architectural; Temple Grove
Colonial Revival (style): elements of, 44, 46, 125. *See also* Bledsoe, L. V., house; Bradley house; Keene house; Mizener house; Revivalism, architectural
Comstock, William C., 20
Comstock house (Eastbank), 20
Cone, Harry C. (contractor): work with Rogers, 49, 99, 129–30
Contractors, 49, 75, 111, 129–30. *See also* Cone, Harry C.
Conway, Lake (Orlando): Huttig house on, 117. *See also* Huttig house
Coquina (stone), 52, 84, 157n1
Corps of Engineers, U.S. Army, 33–35
Costain, Harold Haliday (photographer), 26, 54, 99
Cracker house (type), 30, 46–47. *See also* Regionalism, architectural
Cram, Ralph Adams (architect), 4, 31
Curl, Donald W. (author), *Mizner's Florida,* xvii
Cypress, pecky. *See* Pecky cypress

Daetwyler, Martin J. (landscaper), 49, 82
Daytona Beach, Florida: architects practicing in, 10; Art League of (Daytona Art League), 11; High School, 11–12; JAR practice in, 8–10; Rogers family residence in, 9; Rogers' residential work in, 21; as tourist destination, 9
DeLaHaye, Elias (architect), 10
DeLoe, F. Earl (architect), 27
Depression, Great, 26, 70
Dumbarton Oaks (Washington, D.C.), 63
Dunham, George (architect), 27

Eastbank (Comstock house), 20
École des Beaux-Arts (Paris), 3–4, 5
Edwards, Grace (patron), 27
Elizabeth Drive, 103
Elliott, John M. (architect), xvii
Emery, Don J. (artist), 11
Ergood house, 82
Espedahl, Jacob (architect), 10

Fern Park, Florida: development of, 23–
26, 49, 56; Post Office, 23, 23, 100;
A. T. Traylor house, 23–25, 24; Smith
house, 25
Flagler, Henry: Cordova Hotel (St. Au-
gustine), 40; Florida East Coast Railway, xvii, 9, 45; Whitehall (mansion),
xvii
Florida Architecture and Allied Arts
(magazine), 27, 99, 130
Florida Association of Architects, Sixth
District, publications of, 155–56n11
Florida Bureau of Historic Resources,
xviii
Florida East Coast Railway, xvii, 9, 45.
See also Flagler, Henry
Florida real estate boom, xvi–xvii,
shoddy construction during, 28–29;
collapse of, 56–57; post–World War II,
36. See also Boosterism; Tourism, in
Florida
Florida State Board of Architecture,
xviii, 15–16, 28
Florida Supreme Court Building (Tallahassee), 38–40, 39
Follett, William B. and Edna (patrons),
21, 26–27
Four Winds [Rogers house]: illustrations,
25, 57, 59, 61; discussion of, 25–26,
53–54, 56–62, 69, 100, 117; design of,
59–61; description of, 60–62; alterations to, 61; demolition of, 62. See
also French Provincial (style)
French Provincial (style): elements of,
22–23, 45–46; Rogers' preference for,
59. See also Camp house; Fern Park;
Four Winds; Harris house; Ingram
house; Revivalism, architectural;
Traylor, A. T., house

Friends of Casa Feliz, 82
Fritz, Irwin W. (P.E.), 41

Gamble Rogers Folk Festival, 41
Ganiere, George Etienne (sculptor), 80,
82, 158n2
Garnett, C. E. (architect), 10
Georgia Avenue, 126
Great Depression, 26, 70
Greek Revival, 30–31. See also Classical
Revival; Temple Grove
Greene, Ray (patron), 36–38, 124
Greeneda Court (mixed-use develop-
ment): color plate 1; description of,
37–38. See also Greene, Ray
Griffin, Harry M. (architect), 10
Grinnan, James A. (P.E.), 41
Gwinn, Ralph W., 79–80

Hake, Louis, 30
Hale, Herbert D. (architect), 5
Hare, D. Harold (architect), 27, 28, 129
Harkness, Edward S. (patron of JGRI), 5
Harkness Memorial Quadrangle (Yale
University), 5, 6
Harkness Tower (Yale University), 5, 6
Harris, Percival (patron), 100. See also
Harris house
Harris house: illustrations, 100, 101
(plan), 102; description of, 100–103
Hatton, L. A. (architect), 27
Highlands County Jail, 36
Hitt, Laurance W. (architect), 40, 126,
130
Holabird, William (architect), 2
Holt, George (patron), 32; 103–4, 106–7.
See also Holt house
Holt, Hamilton (president of Rollins
College; patron), 21, 31, 32, 103
Holt, Rebecca (patron), 103–4. See also
Holt house
Holt house: illustrations, 105 (plan), 106
(plan), color plates 4, 5, 6; description
of, 103, 104–7; alterations to, 105–7.
See also Holt, George
Hotel Alabama, 18–20
House Beautiful (magazine): 52, 62; pub-
lication of Rogers' work in, 22; Small

House Competition (1929), 22; influence of, 125
Huttig house, 117, *131*
Hyer, David B. (architect), 15–16

"Ideal for the Small Southern Town, An" (Rogers article), 53
Ingram, L. C. (patron), 96. *See also* Ingram house
Ingram house, 96–99; illustrations, *98, 99*
Interlachen Avenue: Barbour house on, 49, 69; Noyes house on, 85. *See also* Barbour house; Noyes house
International Style, elements of, 111. *See also* Leonard house; Stone, Edward Durell (architect)
Isle of Sicily [Bear Island; Woo Island], development of, 25–26, 57–58, 117. *See also* Burress house; Four Winds; Maitland, Lake

James Gamble Rogers, Inc., 5
Jenney, Major William LeBaron (architect), 2, 154n7
Jenney and Mundie (architecture firm), 2
Jewett, Eugene (patron), 107–8, 111. *See also* Jewett house [Tree Tops]
Jewett, Zoe Shippen. *See* Shippen, Zoe
Jewett house [Tree Tops]: illustrations, *108 (plan), 109, 110, color plate 7*; description of, 107, 108–11. *See also* Shippen, Eugene; Shippen, Zoe

Keene, R. D. (patron), 130. *See also* Keene house
Keene house (Orlando), *129*, 130
Keiser, George Camp (architect), 15, 27, 130
Kiehnel, Richard (architect), xvii, 31
Kiehnel and [John M.] Elliott (architects), 31
Knowles Avenue, 35, 82–83
Korean War: Rogers' service in, 34–35
Kressly, Maurice G. (architect), 27, 129

Lake Adair. *See* Adair, Lake
Lake Conway (Orlando). *See* Conway, Lake

Lake Maitland. *See* Maitland, Lake
Lake Osceola. *See* Osceola, Lake
Lake Virginia. *See* Virginia, Lake
Laurel Avenue (Orlando), 96
Lay, Tracy (patron), 91
Leonard, Dan, 12, 26, 112
Leonard, Edgar Cotrell (patron), 26, 111–12, 116. *See also* Leonard house
Leonard, Emily Nicoll (patron), 112. *See also* Leonard house
Leonard house: illustrations, *112, 114, 115, 116*; siting of, 113; description of, 113–16; alterations to, 111, 117. *See also* Leonard, Edgar Cotrell
Lewis, Sinclair (author), 26, 70
Lincoln Avenue, 35
Lindsey, Harry L. (architect), 27
Lovelock, Ralph (architect), 38, 40

Maitland, Lake: 17; Hotel Alabama on, 18–20; Temple Grove estate on, 20; view from Four Winds, 60; Shippen house on, 62; Harris house on, 100; Jewett house on, 108; Burress house on, 117–19; Mizener house on, 125–26, 128. *See also* Isle of Sicily
Marks Street (Orlando), 96
Marriott, Alvin A. (painter), 129–30
McAllaster, Archibald and Lena (patrons), 91. *See also* McAllaster house
McAllaster house: illustrations, *91, 92 (plan), 93, 94, 97*; description of, 91–97, 99
McCree, W. A. (contractor), 49
Miller, Kenneth (architect), 27
Mills Library. *See* Rollins College
Mizener, Mildred Wells (patron), 125–26. *See also* Mizener house
Mizener house: illustrations, *127 (plan), color plates 13, 14*; siting of, 126; description of, 124, 126–29. *See also* Mizener, Mildred Wells
Mizner, Addison (architect): influence on Florida architecture, xvi–xviii, 48; Everglades Club (Palm Beach), xvii; use of regional materials, 157n1
Mizner's Florida (Curl), xvii

"Modern Jail for Small County" (Rogers article), 36
Moore, Jack (architect), 27
Morse, Charles Hosmer, 20
Morse Avenue, 18
Mundie, William Bryce (architect), 2
Murphy, Robert (architect), 27

National Register of Historic Places, xviii
Newcomb, Rexford, *The Spanish House for America*, 48, 52, 71–72, 87
New England Avenue, 92
New York Avenue, 108
Noyes house: illustrations, *85, 87, 88, 89 (plan)*; discussion of, 85–91; description of, 87–91; addition to, 91. *See also* Noyes, Mabel
Noyes, George Loftus (patron), 85–86. *See also* Noyes house
Noyes, Mabel (patron), 80, *81*, 86, 89. *See also* Noyes house

Oklawaha County, Florida, 41
Old England Avenue, 111, 113
Olin Library. *See* Rollins College
Ormond Beach, Florida, 21–23. *See also* Camp house
Osceola, Florida, 17
Osceola, Lake, 17; "old" Seminole Hotel on, 18–19, *19*; "new" Seminole Hotel on, 18; Comstock house [Eastbank] on, 20; The Palms on, 20; Barbour house on, 70; McAllaster house on, 92; Holt house on, 104, 106; Plant house on, 121; Temple Grove estate on, 30
Osceola Avenue, 112
Osceola Lodge, 20–21

Palm Beach, Florida, xvii. *See also* Mizner, Addison
Palmer Avenue, 20, 121, 125–26
Palms, The, 20
Park Avenue: view of, *18*; Old Post Office on (Rogers office), 35–36, 49, 83; retail development of, 36–38, 84; *Aux Tours D'Argent* (Noyes design shop)

on, 89; Shippen house on, 62; Jewett house [Tree Tops] on, 107–8. *See also* Greeneda Court
Pecky cypress, 52, 67, 157n1. *See also* Regionalism, architectural
Pelton, Henry C. (architect), 7
Penney, J. C. (James Cash), 79–80
Penney Farms (Jacksonville), 79–80, 95
Philips, Charles A. (architect), 5
Plant, Caroline Griggs (patron), 121, 124. *See also* Plant house
Plant, Henry: development of South Florida railroad, xvii, 17; "old" Seminole Hotel, 18
Plant house: illustrations, *123 (plan)*, color plates *11, 12*; siting of, 52–53; description of, 121–24
Provincial Houses in Spain (1925), 48

Railroad. *See* Flagler, Henry; Florida East Coast Railway; Plant, Henry; South Florida Railroad
Regionalism, architectural: climatic considerations, 44, 46–48, 52–53; materials, building, 27, 52, 157n1. *See also* Coquina; Cracker house; Pecky cypress; Penney Farms; Rogers, James Gamble, II, philosophy of architectural design
Revivalism, architectural: Gothic, 4, 31; Tudor, 4; in collegiate architecture, 5–6; Rogers', xvi–xvii, 44–50. *See also* Classical Revival; Colonial Revival; French Provincial; Greek Revival; Spanish; Spanish Eclectic; Spanish Mission; Tudor Revival
Reynolds, Raymond A. (contractor), 49
Rogers, Ann Tift Day (wife of JGRI), 4
Rogers, Elizabeth Hart Baird (wife of JAR), 8
Rogers, Evelyn Claire Smith (wife of JGRII), 15, *16*, 30, *30*
Rogers, Francis D. (architect; son of JGRI), 7
Rogers, Gamble, Folk Festival, 41
Rogers, James Gamble, I (JGRI): portrait of, *3*; biography, 1–7; education, 2–4;

early career in Chicago, 2–3; architectural practice with John Arthur Rogers, 3–4; architectural practice in New York, 5–7; and the Architecture of Pragmatism (Betsky), 2; architectural works, 3, 4–7; death of, 7

Rogers, James Gamble, II (JGRII): portraits of, *iii*, *42*, *54*; biography, 11–16; education, 11–13; attends Dartmouth, 12–13, *13*, 14; joins father's architectural practice, 13–16; moves to Winter Park, 16; engagement and marriage to Evelyn Claire Smith, 15, 16; architectural registration (license), 15–16; opens own firm, 16; president, Mid-Florida AIA chapter, 28; service in the Corps of Engineers, 33–35; military designs, 33–35; jail designs, 36; design for Florida Supreme Court building, 38–40; Florida A&M College, design, 38; publication of work, 24, 25, 36, 28–29, 46, 53, 62; growth of architectural firm and establishment of RLF, 35–41; social connections, 26; retrospectives, 42; death of, 43; influence on regional architecture, 51–55; philosophy of architectural design, 44, 53–54. *See also* Awards; Four Winds [Rogers house]; Temple Grove

Rogers, James Gamble, III, FAIA (son of JGRI; architect), 7, 30

Rogers, James Gamble, IV ("Jimmy"; "Gamble"; son of JGRII), 30, 41; in family portrait, *30*

Rogers, John Arthur (JAR; father of JGRII): portrait of, *10*; biography, 7–11; education, 7; early career, 7–12; practice with James Gamble Rogers I in Chicago, 3–4, 7–8; architectural practice in Chicago, 7–8; moves to Florida, 8; architectural practice in Daytona Beach, 8–10; WWI naval service, 9; architectural works, 10; artwork of, 11; branch office in Winter Park, 15–16, 70; death of, 11, 16; closing of architectural office, 16

Rogers, John Hopewell ("Jack"; son of JGRII): in family portrait, *30*, 30, 41

Rogers, Joseph Martin (grandfather of JGRII): architectural dabbling, 1; biography, 153n1; retires to Seabreeze, Florida, 1

Rogers, Lovelock, and Fritz, Inc. (architecture firm), 41

Rogers, Philips, and Woodyatt (architecture firm), 8

Rogers and Butler (architecture firm), 7

Rogers and Philips (architecture firm), 8

Rogers and Woodyatt (architecture firm), 8

Rogers family: genealogy, 1, 7–8, 11, 15, 153n4; in Chicago, 1–8; and sailing, 11; portrait of, 30. *See also* entries for individual family members

Rogers House (hotel), 17

Rogers house. *See* Four Winds; Temple Grove

Rollins, Alonzo, 17. *See also* Rollins College

Rollins College: establishment of, 17; architectural styles of, 21, 31–32; Olin Library, xv, 31–32, *33*, *42*; faculty, 32; Hamilton Holt as president of, 21, 31, 32; Kiehnel and Elliott, architects for, 31; Knowles Memorial Chapel (Cram), 31; visited by Sinclair Lewis, 26; Mills Memorial Library, 31, 32; Morse Gallery of Art, 27, 55; Spanish-style architectural designs for, 31–32; Spohn, George, architect for, 31; Rogers' architectural designs for, 31–32

Root, John Wellborn (architect), 2

Sailing: Rogers family and, 11; 28; *Jolly Roger* (boat), 28; *Caprice* (boat), 29, 29–30; through hurricane, 29–30

Seabreeze, Florida, 1, 8

Seminole County, Florida, 23

Seminole Hotel: new, 18–19; old, 18, *19*

Shippen, Elizabeth Herrick Blount (patron), 63. *See also* Shippen house

Shippen, Eugene (patron), 62–64, 157n11. *See also* Shippen house

Shippen, Zoe (patron), 64, 107–8, 111. *See also* Jewett house

Shippen house: illustrations, 65, 66 (plan), 67, color plates 2, 3; siting of, 64–65; description of, 64–68. See also Shippen, Eugene

Silsbee, Joseph Lyman (architect), 7–8

Smith, Dorothy Lockhart, xv, 27

Smith, Rhea Marsh, xv, 27

South Florida Railroad, 17. See also Florida real estate boom; Tourism, in Florida

Spanish (style): elements of, 48; Everglades Club (Palm Beach), xvii; University Club, 21; Rogers' appreciation of, 44, 47–48, 155n4; Spanish Farm Houses and Minor Public Buildings (1924), 48; The Spanish House for America (Newcomb), 48, 52; Provincial Houses in Spain (1925), 48. See also Barbour house; Revivalism, architectural; Rollins College; Shippen house

Spanish Colonial (style), elements of, 44–45, 48. See also Revivalism, architectural; St. Augustine

Spanish Eclectic (style), elements of, 45, 47, 62, 68. See also Holt house; McAllaster house; Noyes house; Revivalism, architectural

Spanish Farm Houses and Minor Public Buildings (1924), 48

Spanish House for America, The (Newcomb), 48, 52, 71–72, 87

Spanish Mission (style), 64, 66

Spohn, George (architect), 31

St. Augustine, Florida, xvii, 40. See also Spanish Colonial (style)

St. Johns County, Florida, 40

Stone, Edward Durell (architect): influence on Leonard house design, 113

Sullivan, Louis (architect), 2

Swoope Avenue: Barbour Apartments on, 82; Noyes house on, 85, 87, 89

Tappan, Walter H., house, 128

Taylor County Jail, 36

Temple, W. C., 20

Temple Grove (estate), 20; Rogers family portrait at, 30; Rogers family moves to, 30–31, 62; Rogers designs house at, 30; residential development of, 31

Temple orange, 20, 30

Termite Control (Rogers article), 28–29

Tiedtke, John, 120

Tiedtke house. See Burress house

Tourism: in Florida, xvii, 9, 17–20, 45

Traylor, A. T., house (Fern Park), 24, 25

Tree Tops. See Jewett house

Trowbridge, Alexander Buel, Jr. (patron), 32

Tudor Revival (style), elements of, 4, 31, 117. See also Burress house [Tiedtke house]; Revivalism, architectural

Unitarian Church (Orlando), 64

University Club, 21

Urban, Joseph (architect), xvii

U.S. Army Corps of Engineers, Wilmington District, 33–35

Via Lugano, 100

Virginia, Lake, 46; Bledsoe house on, 46–47, 47; Rogers House (hotel) on, 17

Virginia Inn [Rogers House] (hotel), 17, 18

Waterman, William H. (contractor), 49

Webster Avenue, 18, 21

Whitworth, Henry (architect), 27

Winter Park: Architecturally Winter Park (magazine), 27; architectural identity of, 50, 51–55; Boat Club, 27; development of, 17–21, 18, 19, 155n1; Loring Chase and, 17–18; Oliver E. Chapman and, 17–18; Improvement Association (Chamber of Commerce), 17–18; early map of, 19; chosen as site for Rollins College, 17; Historical Society, 41; hotels, 17–20; incorporation of, 20; preservation ordinance, xviii; Public Library, xv; Register of Historic Places, xviii; Women's Club of, xv, 21, 28

Winter Park Portrait: The Story of Winter Park and Rollins College (Campen), xv

Winter Park Topics (newspaper), 64

Woo Island. *See* Isle of Sicily
World's Columbian Exposition of 1893 (Chicago), 3, 7–8
World War I: effect on Florida, xvii, 45; John Arthur Rogers, service in, 9
World War II: James Gamble Rogers I, service in, 32–35; effect on building industry, 32; postwar boom, 36

Wright, Frank Lloyd (architect), 4, 7
Wyeth, Marion Sims (architect), xvii

Yale University, 3, 5–6, 6
Yellin, Sam (metalsmith), 154n19
Yonge and Hart (architecture firm), 38
Youtsey, J. C., & Co. (plasterers), 129–30

Patrick W. McClane, a native Floridian, worked in the firm of Rogers, Lovelock, and Fritz from 1984 to 1986, while James Gamble Rogers II was still active in the firm. He is a principal architect with Smith and McClane Architects in Richmond, Virginia.

Debra A. McClane worked for the Historic Tampa/Hillsborough County Preservation Board in Tampa from 1992 to 1994. She is a private consultant in architectural history and historic preservation.